Mark Mills Pomeroy

Sense, or, Saturday-night musings and thoughtful papers

Mark Mills Pomeroy

Sense, or, Saturday-night musings and thoughtful papers

ISBN/EAN: 9783337084196

Printed in Europe, USA, Canada, Australia, Japan

Cover: Foto ©ninafisch / pixelio.de

More available books at **www.hansebooks.com**

Just Published,

A new Book, uniform with this Volume, and Illustrated, entitled

Nonsense,

BY

"BRICK" POMEROY.

⁎ *These books are sold everywhere, and will be sent by mail,* POSTAGE FREE, *on receipt of price,* $1.50,

BY

G. W. Carleton & Co., Publishers, New York.

SENSE,

OR

Saturday-night Musings and Thoughtful Papers.

BY

"BRICK" POMEROY,

(*Editor of the La Crosse, Wis., Democrat.*)

WIT

NEW YORK:
G. W. Carleton & Co., Publishers.
LONDON: S. LOW, SON & CO.
MDCCCLXVIII.

Entered according to Act of Congress, in the year 1869, by
G. W. CARLETON & CO.,
In the Clerk's Office of the District Court of the United States for the Southern District of New York.

81, 83, *and* 85 *Centre Street,*
NEW YORK.

Dedication.

To men who have *souls*—
To young men of *ambition*—
To those who have *hearts*—
To all who would be better and happier—
To my earnest friends everywhere—

THIS, MY FIRST VOLUME,

Is most respectfully dedicated by the Author,

M. M. POMEROY.

LA CROSSE, WIS., 1867.

CONTENTS.

CHAPTER	PAGE
I.—A Few Remarks about the Road of Life	9
II.—The Magic Artist	19
III.—In which People are Spoken to Sensibly	32
IV.—In which Little Boys and Big Boys are Told to Think	38
V.—A Letter from Home	45
VI.—We Reason Together on Success	51
VII.—Saturday Night	58
VIII.—In which Easy Lessons are Given Out	63
IX.—The Evening Star	70
X.—In which Disappointment is Favorably Mentioned	77
XI.—Wherein Common-Sense is Entitative	85
XII.—In which we Speak about Pluck	91
XIII.—Knitting	97
XIV.—We Walk in the Cold, and Pity where Others Condemn	103
XV.—Wherein the Use of Eyes is Looked Over	110
XVI.—In which we Find Smiles among Tears	119
XVII.—A Short Talk about how to Get Along	126
XVIII.—Fireside Musings	132
XIX.—In which we Speak of the Roads, the Hearth and Fender	138
XX.—Sunday Night	147
XXI.—In which we Travel on Dangerous Ground	150
XXII.—About Twigs and their Early Bending	159
XXIII.—In which a Hard Word is Used	168
XXIV.—Musings at the End of the Week	173
XXV.—In which Post-Mortem Processions are Spoken of	178
XXVI.—Pictures	185
XXVII.—We Wonder why Wonders will never Cease!	192
XXVIII.—Wherein the Use of Money is Spoken of	199
XXIX.—For Married Men, and their Wives	205
XXX.—Boys and Apprentices are Spoken of and to	212
XXXI.—My Boy is Counselled to Mind his own Business	219
XXXII.—We Speak of Something that Concerns Somebody	225
XXXIII.—We Converse on how Men may Succeed	232
XXXIV.—We Talk of Things we ought not to Talk of	238
XXXV.—We find Where to Look for Happiness	243
XXXVI.—Another Week Gone	249
XXXVII.—Happy New Year	257
XXXVIII.—Saturday Night	267

PREFACE.

I DO not understand it!
Who of us does?
Do you?
There is something so much beyond human reasoning in this life, that one hardly dares to stop thinking long enough to think! It is so terrible to be lost! And there is so much, and yet so little, that who of us has the courage to stop, even in thought, beyond the present. So many have gone before, yet they tell us nothing, and we play like children waiting the bell!

It seems as though we could make the path to the school-room door an easier one to walk in if we would. If we but took half the pains to shun the brambles and ugly points we take to run upon them, how easy would be the road! And thus it is that we at night loosen the curtains, tone the light, draw the easy-chair to hearth and fender, forget the world, and run the pen, line upon line, doing to others as we would have them do by us.

Who cares for any of us?
No one!
Do we care for ourselves?
No!

And yet we do. We all look for the pearls of time, half dark, half light, as HE sends them to us for such purpose as we will—days we save or lose. Let us not condemn the day till we have seen its sunset—let those who read these pages not condemn till the pages have all been turned. Life is but acts. Books are but leaves. All in all, and thus the summing.

Looking backward, we see a winding path, reaching back into a narrow labyrinth of uncertainty—now opening wider and wider into a plain of beauty and hours of happiness as we journey on the *Road to Life*, never fearing the reward, never holding back a step, lest it be the one that marks our mile-stone! We see in the path behind us a poor boy alone, struggling with fate, trials, poverty, and life's temptations, with no one to aid him kindly. To be sure, hands were outreached; but they often were cold, and the words spoken lacked earnest meaning.

We have often hungered for some one who knew the road to walk with us, and teach us how to give vigor to step, and something more than a tiresome aim to life. We have often wished for some one to do by us as we will do by them; so we sit quietly by the table, and with never a thought of wrong, but a heart full of love to all—be they the boys like VALTER, our young companion, who listens as we talk of life—men like ourself, who may, and may not, think of thoughts which run from brain to pen-point as we write, or those of either sex whose dark hours, whose sad hours—whose longing hours have been many, yet whose days have been bright, and would have been more so if those who make the world had done by them as we would have done by them.

So do not throw this little volume down lightly.

It will do you no harm.

It assumes no dictation.

It is not a refrigerator to congeal and keep within you the legacy of sin we inherited.

It is simply the honest, home-like talk of a walker on life's road, to be read by the youth who need friends—by the middle-aged who have none too many—by the ones who do and who do not see more of their loved ones by the hearth and fender—by those who would be happy, yet in the bustle of life have no time to ask of those who have not been in such haste to travel the road VALTER and us set out to walk.

M. M. POMEROY.

SANCTUM OF "DEMOCRAT," *La Crosse, Wis.*, 1867.

"As you are a boy, so will you be a man, Valter. The golden crop cannot be garnered till after the grain has been sown."—*Page 9.*

Sense.

CHAPTER I.

A Few Remarks about the Road of Life.

WALTER, my boy, we are walking along. The road turns now to the right, then to the left. It is not altogether smooth, yet we can pick our way along and not stumble if we heed where we set our feet. There are brambles thick set along the road—their points stand ready to lacerate all who would force their way through without regard for proper paths.

And there are others on this same road—some are old with us—more are young with you.

It is useless, Valter, to ask where *they* are going, when we know not where we are bound to. All we have to do, my boy, is to walk on—and on—and on. The road will end somewhere. It will lead us by many beautiful places, and past many treacherous grounds. It will lead us by churches — cradles — hearses—weddings—happy homes—broken hearts tossed high on limbs of loveless trees—old people and young people—weddings and funerals. It will lead us, my boy, up steep paths where none but the bold dare tread, to summits from which we can look down upon the world at labor, or it will lead us down slippery places, into life's swamps, from whose miry depths it will be very hard to retrace our steps.

The road opens—it narrows. Its sides converge or diverge as we look. It leads to a broad plain where men are brothers and heart beats true to heart, and where the sunlight of GOD's wondrous love germinates love and spiritual fragrance, or into little, narrow prison-houses of mind, dank and lonesome.

It is but a step from one end of this road to the other, Valter—yet it is a hard road to walk. The priest and christening are back of us, my boy. The cradle is small, Valter, but there is always more room in it than in the largest coffin. The minister baptizes you in the morning—he marries you at noon—he reads a funeral sermon at night—and is ready for the morrow. The road ends. You fall out by the way violently, or walk out and on the broad plain at the end of the road quietly.

There are flowers and beauties on the road, but few of us see them, my boy. There are hidden beauties which must be sought out—there are countless bowers behind the brambles—there are mossy banks at the foot of many of these old oaks, where friends can sit and be happy. We run from the cradle to the grave, reaching for some hand in the distance—stepping to gain a foothold on some vessel far out at sea, swiftly flying still farther from us. Life is in living. Death is not in dying. Life is not the dazzling sun, but the countless stars which twinkle and flash— GOD's diamonds that they are. The sun is not beautiful, though it be grand. Far more beauty in the pleiades. Life is in the little acts—the good intentions — the purity of our motives. Death is the memory we leave behind us for others.

But few of our hopes are ever realized, Valter. It is in fancy that we revel in love and find happiness in places here and there. How the dreams recede! The lips are not so sweet forever as once. The heart is at times something besides a harmonious harp. The song of love dies out, and there sweep over the soul storms of passion, dark shadows driven by fierce blasts, old memories dragging their slow lengths like wounded sunbeams, to keep pace with us to the grave. The cloud is not solid, and he who would ride thereon must first become immortal. And we make our own immortality, Valter.

Labor for happiness. The marble palace is not always the bower of love. The rustling silk does not always herald affection. Wealth is not riches more than old age is experience. By the humble cottage-fire is happiness. The hand of the honest laborer, calloused though it be, is softer than many a palm kid touched to-day. The smile that beams on the face of the occupant of that little cabin hidden by the woods, as his little ones run to meet him when the labors of the day are over, is truer and has more of God's sunshine in it than a thousand peals of laughter from gas-lit halls and sumptuous parlors. The loftiest tree does not bear the sweetest fruit. The highest bough is not the most secure home for the bird that sings our sorrows away. The hand of a poor man, Valter, is the hand of an honest one—the heart of a poor man, my boy, is the safest shelter in time of storm—the tongue of the laborer, no matter how broken or what its language, is generally the tongue of truth, and its rhythm more in unison with heavenly harmony than most of us dream of. Tears come from the poor man's heart. Smiles come therefrom also, and they are true and warm.

In a little while the end of the road will open before us. A sudden turn or gentle winding will reveal our home. Then we lie down as others have before us, on the *right or left* as we shall choose. And the man who prayed at our christening will preach at our burial. The birds we see overhead will sing as sweetly as now, and rear their young with the same care. The sun will laugh, the stars will smile, the zephyrs play among the boughs—the leaves will dance over our graves —the rain patter upon our earthly roof as if in mockery, and weeds or flowers spring into life and perfume as we shall take seeds with us into the grave. And those who now laugh with us will laugh without us. A few tears will be shed, and the fountains of grief will then be dried up. The sun will shine as usual. The morn, and the noon, and the night will come. The lips we have kissed, others will kiss. The hand we have clasped, another will hold—the heart we have nestled in will open for another, and the wondrous links in the chain of life will still be as complete as though we had never been. The eyes which now in love answer back will soon smile to cheer another heart. The books and things we love will be thrown aside—the hopes we had in childhood will fade like shadows—the loves of riper years will be comforted after we are GONE HOME—the hearth and fender now our own will be another's. The cloud of grief may bring a storm—a tempest, but storms and tempests will pass away, and the places of earth that now know you, Valter, will know you only through your good or evil deeds, and the name you leave behind. The world will exist long after we are gone. The road will be travelled long after our footprints are forgotten.

Then, Valter, my boy, let us mellow the mould all we can. Every good act is a flower which will beautify our final home. Every good deed is an evergreen which will mark our resting-place. Every good intention is a bird which will sing the harmony of love over our grave. Every pure motive will be a screen to beat back the hot sun of calumny, and every friend we are true to will be a witness for us when the hour comes when we shall want them.

Do not stop, my boy, to pick up that crooked stick by the roadside. Step over it. Let it lie. It is a dirty, vulgar stick we will admit, but do not disturb it. Let it remain where it is, and soon the green grass will grow up around it— the violet and dandelion will bloom beside it— the wild rose will reach its tiny arms over it and wave its perfumed breath back and forth, filling the air with the aroma of innocence. Let it lie. Some people hurl ugly sticks without an object. They do not hurl them to clear the road, but to cause some one else to stumble. To pull one out from its half-hidden place, is to pull up the plants which are weaving the mantle of forgetfulness over its deformities, and leave an ugly scar on the green sward beneath which we must some day rest. Hurl it where you will—into the river, and it floats on to lodge somewhere. Hurl it to the right or left and it falls to the earth—breaking down innocent grass, mangling tender flowers, breaking the life out of stamen, leaf, and pistil—destroying beauty which should be spared for other purposes. Let the crooked acts—the gnarled sticks lie where they fell, Valter. The plants will soon hide them—they will decay and give new life through God's changes, to please and beautify. All through the grass—on either side the road are twigs, sticks, and broken limbs. Walk on, Valter, and over them.

If any one has stumbled and fallen, help him up gently and pass on before a crowd gathers.

Open your eyes—open your heart—expand your ideas and be more of a man. Be true to your word—to yourself. Do by others as you would have them do by you, and this becomes a pleasant road in which to walk, Valter, my boy.

CHAPTER II.

THE MAGIC ARTIST.

HE spirits and fairies held high carnival in front of the house last night, and this morning the windows presented the most beautiful sight I ever beheld. While those indoors were sleeping, winter had set its spring patterns for summer work, and how delicate were the touches and tracings of its magic pencil! One window, in particular, presented the most beautiful sight I ever saw. It seemed as though a convention of angel artists had been summoned by the dying Winter-king, and, by the light of the *aurora*

borealis, had made him a picture of such magic beauty, that no one could look upon it without feeling to do him homage. There were the bold, heavy strokes of some rough old frost-spirit who delighted in making mountains, rocks, cascades, and deep ravines. There stood the work of less dashing artists, delighting in the production of plains, rivers, oceans, and deserts. Then there were panes filled with forests deep and dark— with woods rivalling the famed Bois de Boulogne —with prairies and deserts stretching off into the distance, till lost in touches so delicate that the breath of a spirit even, must drive the work away. There were sketches by gentler artists, of birds, of plants, of flowers, and a thousand beautiful fancies. There were the choicest, most delicate embroideries, rivalling the finest Honiton, so neatly woven, of so fine a texture, and of such handsome patterns that it seemed as if the wedding lace and bridal veils of angels had been stolen from their heavenly wardrobe, and placed on the window before me to teach man his utter insignificance.

The entire panorama of sea—of earth—of air—of Heaven and of Eternity, lay spread out there, and countless thousands of more beautiful pictures were presented than artist ever saw in his most golden dreams. Cities, teaming with life; streets filled with horses, carriages, and pedestrians, crossing, passing, and repassing each other; blocks of stores, in the windows of which could be seen all that makes up the wardrobe of the most fashionable lady or gentleman, or the coarser habiliments of poverty. There were blocks of tenement-houses, the roofs broken in and walls toppling—the doors unhinged and windows shattered—leaning and nodding toward each other as if mocking at the misery of their inmates!

There were cities silent and deserted, with battered walls, crumbling houses, ruined churches and streets, looking silent, and filled with rubbish. There were cities filled with handsome residences, splendid parks in which were fountains—churches built after a score of architectural designs, the spires losing themselves in the midst of countless glittering stars, each pointing to heaven as the source of inspiration. Groups of people—flocks of birds—of water-fowl, and herds of horses were to be seen. There were trees growing up straight and handsome, the upper limbs heavy with foliage —trees gnarled and twisted as is the life of the friendless—trees laden with tropical fruits—trees in whose branches could be seen beautiful "feathered" birds—trees under which could be seen lovers fondly reclining—trees in which serpents were writhing and swinging from branch to branch, and trees beneath which were groups of cattle, apparently enjoying the shade a capricious puff of wind had thrown from the thickly woven branches! Oh, how beautiful!

Mountains reared their lofty summits till the highest peaks seemed lost in the antechamber of heaven, and adown whose sides hung frozen cascades. There were towers rivalling Bunker Hill, the Washington Monument, the leaning tower of Pisa, or the tower of Babel! There were plains on which deer, wild horses, cattle, and buffalo roamed and raced and sported in all their native freedom. Flower gardens had been cultivated there, so perfect that on the different variety of shrubs and plants could be seen leaves, stems, flowers, and buds, with humming-birds and butterflies lightly hovering thereon. There were forests interlaced with walks, and filled in with tangled thickets, from which protruded heads of wild boars, of tigers, of hyenas, of toads, of serpents, and of devils! There were little waterfalls leaping from rock to rock, or pouring over abrupt cliffs, losing themselves in the spray which fell on the tree-tops below, or rising in a cloud of stars, glittering like diamonds 'neath the rays of the rising sun!

Then came lakes and oceans on whose bosoms could be seen ships sailing smoothly along, or plunging madly over the rolling waves before a howling tempest! There were rivers covered with various craft, along whose banks walked students with their books, philosophers with their thoughts, speculators with their plans, hypocrites with their promises, children with their playmates, lovers with their hopes: and dancing, grinning devils following after, overtaking here and there a poor victim who had been abandoned. There were rivers lying between banks lined with bending grass, or lofty trees, and bluffs reaching so high that it seemed as if their tops were piercing the doom of heaven. Groups by the fireside—bands of angels—crowds of spirits interweaving and interlacing with each other, were pictured out with the greatest accuracy.

There were solitary farm-houses, silent graveyards, lonely chambers, and deserted prisons; there was a battle-field, on which could be seen soldiers engaged in deadly strife with weapons flashing in the sun—warriors, on foot and mounted, rushing hither and thither—horses, madly plunging over the forms of the dead and dying—groups of soldiers bearing off a wounded comrade—officers leading their forlorn hopes—soldiers kneeling in prayer; writhing in agony; engaged in hand-to-hand conflict, and standing sentinel on the outpost—squads of men beside cannon, in front of which lay wreaths of dead or wounded—officers' tents—regiments of men not yet called into action. Over this field hovered ravens and angels, while on it could be seen women guarding and nursing those dearer to them than life itself.

Every artist from the spirit-world must have been engaged here last night. There were implements and machines of all kinds. A printing-press standing beside a guillotine—a cradle beneath a gallows—a violin and case of surgical instruments lay side by side on a card-table—a cannon on which was a pipe of peace, stood boldly forth—a broadsword and quill pen hung suspended from the same hook—a pleasure carriage and an artillery wagon stood ready for use, while in the distance was a railroad on which was a train made up of cars, stages, high-back cutters, wheelbarrows, stone-boats, Chinese ploughs, and Indian dug-outs! And each was perfect, as though these were the patterns from which everything of the kind had been fashioned.

There were crowded ball-rooms—picnic parties roaming through grottos, and resting in sylvan-like retreats and hidden trysting-places. There were preachers holding forth to crowded audiences, composed of bareheaded men and veiled women. There were farm scenes and city scenes. There were sportsmen on the plain in full pursuit of buffalo—soldiers on horses chasing flying Indians—hunters in the forest standing beside a tree, or kneeling behind a log, waiting the approach of a deer, seen in the distance, snuffing danger from afar! Everything that man could think of was here, so beautifully designed, so boldly commenced, so lightly finished, so perfect and so varied, that it seemed as if the whole panorama of eternity had been spread before those who chose to witness the magnificent display. There were libraries filled with books —carriages filled with people—stores filled with goods—the air filled with birds—faces of men, women, and children, filled with joy, hope, fear, love, hate, doubt, sorrow, anguish, remorse, and despair—heavens filled with angels, firmaments studded with stars, each scene glistening, flashing, and glittering under the rays of the morning sun with a far greater brilliancy than ever shone from pearl or diamond! Beautiful and mysterious!

*   *   *   *   *   *

I have just been in to look at the window again, and such a change! My stars have all disappeared; the delicate tracings making the foliage of the forests have all melted down. The beautiful plants are stripped of their leaves and flowers, and look more like straws, broken and twisted into a thousand ugly shapes! The pretty little humming-birds and butterflies have all melted and are not to be seen! The birds, that looked so beautiful half-hidden among the leaves of the trees, are flown, and the little twigs on which they sat have melted off one by one, till all the pretty branches are gone! The lovers are gone from their trysting-places, and the little mounds on which they sat, surrounded by flowers, have been transformed into wet, cold graves! The beautiful pines, from the drooping boughs of which hung such beautiful snow draperies a few moments since, have been breathed on by a passing breeze, and now stand there, gnarled and twisted trunks, devoid of beauty or interest. The splendid embroidery is not to be seen; but where it was so artistically draped and elegantly displayed, hangs something that looks like a shroud! The crowded room in which an hour since so many were dancing, has grown larger, but the dancers have departed! Where the orchestra was, is now a coffin, with but one solitary mourner kneeling by its side, her head bent in weeping, her feet bathed in tears! God bless the solitary one, wherever she may be! The pretty walks and borders in the Bois de Boulogne have given place to sloppy gutters, down which the molten frost is coursing! The mountains are dwindling down—the plains on which so many buffalo were seen, are still there, but oh! how changed! The ships have gone to the bottom of the lakes and oceans, while the oceans are also disappearing! The river that looked so beautiful an hour since is still to be seen, but it is now the river of death! Its swelling waters have flooded the flowery banks—have swept down the little craft that floated so securely there not long since, and are now climbing and washing up against the sides of the bluffs! The battle-field has been drowned in tears, and all that remains of its glittering soldiery, and thirst for glory, is a blank. The spires have gone from the churches—the cities have been drowned out—the streets are little Holland canals—the deer and hunter have sunk into the earth—the crowd that walked by the river bank have all gone, and the whole scene has changed!

The railroad has been taken up, and the train of cars has given way for a hearse in which is a coffin! All the happiness I saw there an hour since has fled, and nothing now is left but tears and *panes!* The little cascades, rivulets, and brooklets have run into a lake, in which I can see a few mounds covered by fiends, leaping and grinning at the general ruin! The angels have departed, but all over the window are the tears they shed at the fall of my miniature world! The tree so laden with fruit has been trimmed of its branches till it resembles a man who has lost his friends, and from whom hope has fled—a twisted, ugly, deformed trunk, fast settling into the general destruction.

* * * * * *

Now *all* is gone! trees, plants, birds, angels, demons, rivers, animals, ships, implements, men, cities, deserts, mountains—all—*all* have melted—a few tears being all that is left of what was once so beautiful. Like some men who by one action can sweep out a life of honor and happiness, so has nature, in one hour, swept away the labor of an entire night, leaving us but the lesson to enjoy the beautiful while it is with us, and that when the ball-room of her life gives way for the room of weeping, we may merit the tears of at least a solitary mourner.

CHAPTER III.

IN WHICH PEOPLE ARE SPOKEN TO SENSIBLY.

AH! my boy, there is not one in a thousand thinks of it—not one in two thousand can remember the lesson after it is taught him or her. Look over the world of nations or of individuals. They who do the best are they who mind their own business. God did not make man double-barrelled. No man can well attend to the business which concerns himself and that which concerns another. If his brain is afflicted with strabismus, somebody must suffer. From the cradle to the grave the same lesson is daily given. Mind your business, Valter, my boy. Keep the rubbish cleared from before your own door. What is the sense of kicking up a row over what concerns you no more than gravestones or their letters concern the dead?

If a man insults you personally, resent it. If he wrongs a friend, stand up for that friend as he would for you. But do not go snooping around, prying with pointed nose into what affects you not. Whose business is it if this neighbor drives a black horse, that neighbor a white one, and your other neighbor goes on foot like a monarch over his own will! Does it affect you if such a man is another's friend or his enemy? It is not your province to harness into quarrels not your own, lest in time you have so many on hand there will be no time to attend to them.

They who are rich are they who mind their own business. Find a happy man or woman, and the affairs of another trouble them but little.

It is none of your business if the minister

kisses one of the sisters, or one of the sisters thus salutes the minister. It cannot affect you, when a man you know calls on a girl you don't know, or on one you do. What if there is kissing behind the door—in tunnels, and when the night is dark, at the vestibule of the church, or over the gate! Would you not do the same if the chance were offered? If a man is making money, is it any of your business, provided he does it honestly? There are a thousand things coming up every day, in which people have no heart. Yet they meddle therewith, as if life or death hung in the balances. Stand up straight. Look to yourself. Do not be an echo. Have a mind of your own or do not take a position. You cannot control heaven or earth, nor the occupants of either. Man was born of God. Each has his rights, as have you. Don't pry. Don't meddle. Don't make a fool of yourself by laying out work you can't do. Go on about your own business, and let others do the same. If a man is in trouble, help him out. Do not help him in. God knows, my boy, life runs to trouble, as clouds do to storms, or gardens to weeds. Try it a week, and see how much lighter the spirit-load when Saturday night comes. Never go out of the way to make a fool of yourself, or to make others miserable. There is need of men of sense now. There always will be need of such. Do not sit gazing out of the window to see what chance there is in the vicinity to raise a row. If you have nothing else to do, go to sleep. Where God makes hearts, man cannot alter the actions of others. Some will laugh— some will weep—some will mourn. Don't worry. It is better to close the eyes at times than to keep them open. Sometimes, my boy, people see too much, and when on the witness-stand embarrass themselves more than others. Don't be envious—or jealous. Don't be governed by spite. Don't believe all that people tell you. There is many a one, my boy, who would make a fool of you. There are thousands of silly stories told which had their origin in idle and lying brains. Don't circulate them. Don't believe them when told of yourself unless they are true. Be what your friends *think* you are—avoid being what your enemies *say* you are, and be happy. Keep your own heart right. Mind your own business and let that of others alone. Do not dig in the ground to find the seed of the pointed thorn that scratches you. Time spent in that manner is lost. Go on. Keep a stiff upper lip—live to please your own heart. No other rests with you in the grave. No other keeps you company in that grand city where each minds his own business. The city of the dead is one of peace and quietness. There, no one interferes with the affairs of his neighbor. There, no petty strifes, quarrels, and bickerings annoy or trouble. What a lesson those silent mounds give. There, each is king over his own tenement, and there is no trouble, because each minds his own business. And Valter, my boy, the world would be thus peaceable if each man and woman in it would learn a lesson. Try it for awhile. Look down into your own heart, my boy. See if there does not arise each day many a chance to breed trouble by meddling with or peddling rumors—many a chance to avoid it by going your way with closer mouth. Each man owes it to himself to make not only himself but others happy—no way can it be done so well and surely as by minding your own business. Remember this, my boy, and your circle of friends will grow larger and your heart lighter, as the invisible pages are turned which bring you nearer to the solving of the great riddle, the key of which is so-called death.

CHAPTER IV.

In which Little Boys and Big Boys are told to Think.

WALTER, my boy, do you ever pause to think? If not, you are at fault, when there is so much to think of. There are millions of ideas yet to be born. There are millions of years yet to live. It may not be on this earth, but we shall live somewhere. The grave is the lock which must be opened before we touch or enjoy the treasures beyond its dark keeping — before we go to the punishments or rewards we plan for in this world. And there is much to think of which concerns this life. As you are a boy, so will you be a man, Valter. The golden crop cannot be garnered till after the grain has been sown. The impression cannot be read till after the type is set in order. And the errors show in the proof. You cannot be a man unless in boyhood you decide to be one. People seldom blunder on success as a blind pig falls into a well. Luck is nothing more than effort well directed. Stones do not of themselves turn up as you pass by to reveal the wealth hidden under them. Men do not often succeed by chance. This world was not made by chance. It was made. Men are made. It takes years to make them. In all sorts of trials, all kinds of troubles—under many trying circumstances the lessons of life are learned. If you would succeed as a man, you must try to excel as a boy. Think! That is the word. Think that a rowdy boy makes a loafer. Think that an idle boy makes a blackguard. Think that a careless boy makes a poor man. Think that a poor man is a slave. Think what others have done, and that it is in your power to do still better if you will. Think that you will some day be a man, and called on to take an active part in life's battles. You will either lead or be led. It lies in you to decide which. Wrinkles creep over the face never to go off. Habits silently but surely creep into your spirit, and you cannot get rid of them. You will some day be a man. Think whether you will be a voter all your life, or be voted for. Think whether you will please those who bid, or bid those you please. Think whether you will be a fretful, disagreeable old man whom every one will wish dead, or a respected old gentleman whose grave will be watered with tears—whose kind words and smiles will be missed—whose precepts or examples will be loved and copied. Think of all these things, my boy.

It is easy to be poor man. All you have to do is to work hard and never think. Work hard and spend foolishly at card-table and in nonsense. Marry in haste and repent at leisure.

"THINK whether you will be a voter all your life, or be voted for."—*Page* 40.

Slide down hill, and walk back drawing your sled after you. If you are poor, run in debt. Keep poor—a slave to every man. If you have a wife and are in debt, keep a hired girl. If in debt with nothing to do, keep two servant-girls. If very poor and in debt, keep two servant-girls and a dog. Keep up style. Fish for fools—bait the hook with the biggest one and you will catch them sure. If you owe a man, cheat him out of the debt. If you can borrow instead of earning, do so. Keep borrowing. Pry into all that concerns you not. Tell all you know. Teach every one to dislike you. Act out nature and be a hog, or think a little and be a man. Life is a show. You can have a hard seat or a cushioned one. The first investment for a ticket decides the matter.

The man who never thinks is a fool. His life is like midnight dreams—morn comes and they are gone. Death comes and the game is over. Fortune does not teaze men to shake her hand.

A good opportunity never waits. If you are not ready, some one else will be. The wheel goes round—the car moves on—if you do not occupy the seat, some one else will. It will not be long before you will be a man, Valter. Then, what will you do?' Whose brains will you use? Do you intend to work all day for just what will last you all night, or have you an idea for the future? Are you doing your best? If not, why not? Think of these things, my boy. Look for bad examples. Shun them. Look for good examples. Imitate them. When you see a man fail, be assured there was a reason. Think and search it out. If he succeeds, learn his secret and follow it. If a man has friends, think how he made them. All friends are made. Relations grow. Friends we make for ourselves. We make them and we love them. Enemies are as necessary to success as vinegar to pickles. They are the long oars, which in sturdy hands shoot the boat, deep though it be laden, far out and clear over the foaming breakers into a smooth sea beyond.

Do not be a hypocrite, my boy. Better be a thief—a robber. Play your hand open. Never wear spectacles to deceive folks. Never profess to do what you do not. Do not be afraid of what others may say—people will talk. Fools will turn grindstones for others to sharpen scythes upon, and fools will talk of that which does not concern them, of what they cannot effect —of that which is none of their business. Think for yourself. Advise with your own heart. Do as best pleases you. Satisfy one man first. Do not promise over a thousand pups out of one litter. He may be a mean man who would not promise a pup to a friend, but he is a meaner man who promises more than he can perform. Do not take four passengers in a wagon intended for but two. Do not try to please everybody and please none. Few people care for you. Fear is stronger than love. But few people will love you. Society thinks you are an orange to be squeezed for its benefit. Think how few people care for Myou. en seldom work except for pay. People are generally friends only while they can lap from your saucer. They eat the corn and throw the cob away.

CHAPTER V.

A Letter from Home.

THE post-mark has a familiar look. The chirography speaks before the envelope is torn off of a letter from home—the dear old home by the brook side many hundred miles away. With eager, trembling hand the welcome token is drawn from its office-marked wrapper, and then how the half-stilled heart drinks the contents! From a mother, or one who in childhood's days filled the place of the loved and dead. Each line breathes the spirit of love, care, friendship, and affection so deeply graven on the tablets of memory. And how visions of the old home come crowding up! The store-house of the past opens to the inner rooms, and down the long aisles of yearly events there looms up pictures varied, sad, joyous, and cherished. We read on, and back to the scenes of childhood the soul rushes like a dove let loose from tangled snare. We see the old house. No palace half so loved. The little yard with here and there a bunch of flowers. The old well into whose depths so oft we gazed as lovers do into each other's eyes. The moss-covered bucket with rusty bands. The little spring in the milk-house. The rows of pans on the rustic bench. The chamber with its well-filled rooms. The parlor kept sacred for company. The table at whose head her of the kind heart and gentle eye so well presided. How large a freight is there on the return trip of memory! The garden with its plants and weeds—its scattered tools and little beds. Out into the old barn. There is the hay-mow where oft we romped with dog and playmates—the red fanning-mill in whose mysterious depths were eggs and nests—the broken-tined pitchfork—the partly toothed rake—the bent-edged scoop—the old-fashioned flail, and hunts under closely packed sheaves for rats and mice. Who does not love a letter from home? A picture of the past—a key to the million of pictures! The little old bookcase with the dog-eared volumes quaint and brown. The hated churn in the cellar. The loft where erst the rattling nuts told of foraging youngsters. The apple-bins and barrels in the cellar. The wagon-house with that old-style buggy—its high back—its small forward and large hind wheels long since obsolete—the old house-dog—the sheep with tinkling bell, heard on the distant hillside—the berry patch wherein us youngsters romped and hunted amid briers and with scratched hands for red-caps and blackberries. The little stream which sang all the night and whistled over pebbly beds all the day. How we loved to catch therefrom the struggling prize. And then the school-house where oft and oft the falling book or slate has called the dreamer back to his work—where childish loves and jealousies were ripened by a glance or buried with a word. How memory comes with her many offerings! Pen fails; words run together as drops of water. Like flowers in one's lap, there is a pile of pictures. There come a thousand fond recollections. The young sweethearts—the struggles for stolen kisses—the dreams of life never realized. The longings and sighings for the future to open its wonderful doors still faster and faster.

And the years come like sentinels, each bringing a mile-post. Children grown into youths. One by one they leave the loved hearth-stone—one by one new faces come and go. There is a marriage here—a funeral there. Which party goes to misery, and which to happiness, none but God knows! The chances are even! The family circle is broken. In the front room—whose stillness is heavy and terrible with dread—lie one after another who have CHANGED before us! The silent step—the careful breathing—the low whisper as the sheet is turned back to show the once warm lips now cold and blue in death. The wondering if we too must die—the crowd of mourners—the slow ride to the grave—the hollow rattle upon the coffin—all come before us like a panorama in detail.

And then, other changes. And, still, other changes. Each bringing a new picture, sometimes golden-lined—oftener black like the storm-cloud which bursts, and growls, and mutters, then rolls its ugly self away to reveal the clear cerulean beyond.

Letters from home! God bless them. Who would be without them? Who would refuse or neglect to write them. When the heart is sad they bring gladness—when all the future and all the present look like midnight, the past comes up, and, conning over the stored pictures, the heart forgets its weariness and wakes to new life—to new hope—to newer love—to stronger faith—to braver courage. A letter from home! More precious than gold—more prized than hopes, for it takes us back to happy hours, and renews the strength for the future.

CHAPTER VI.

WE REASON TOGETHER ON SUCCESS.

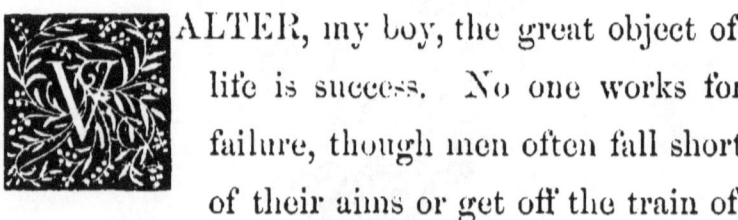

ALTER, my boy, the great object of life is success. No one works for failure, though men often fall short of their aims or get off the train of events a long way before reaching the station. In the silent hours of night — in the lonely and dreamy hours of day, an active brain of earnest man is ever planning some new road to success—some route as yet unexplored. Life is often spent in study, and down to the narrow mansion passes all a man's hopes before he is ready to rest from labor. There are many ways to succeed, my boy, and very many ways to fail. In love or business, in the mighty struggle for wealth or power, there are many lessons to be learned. And, my boy, we have books on medicine, religion, horse-doctoring, curing hams, making farms, railroading, cotton-growing, raising strawberries, necromancy, banking, and a thousand other things. These tell us how to do almost everything—still people fail. There is something wrong. A leak in talent exists somewhere.

Yet it seems as though every one could succeed. No one starts out in life with other intentions; but, my boy, the road becomes too long at the other end for many a brave youth —for many a stout-hearted man. There are little lessons to be learned. There are small wheels to machinery as well as large ones. Life is a complicated invention. Little things are many times overlooked till too late. We notice the man without looking at his eyes. We see the dollar without looking at the penny. We fail, my boy, for the lack of some little pin or connection passed by as worthless. Every failure in life has a starting-point, as every tree which breaks had first to bend; as every river was first a spring. Let us look out for the small items; larger ones will take care of themselves.

God, in His wisdom, gave us different ideas. If we had all been made alike—if each had the same tastes, this world would have been like a fine-toothed comb. We should have built houses alike, worn clothes alike, and been like a basket of eggs on general principles. Then every man would have loved the same woman—and what a row that one thing would have kicked up! All other women would have been jealous; all the men would have been fighting; the one woman would be poisoned or slandered to death by her sex—the men would kill each other off in battle on her account, and a nation of old maids would be left desolate.

There is a way, Valter, my boy, to do everything. First open shop. Make up your mind what to do. Then shun the bridges others fell through. If you promise to do a thing, do it. If you do a man a kindness, do it with a pleasant face. A little vinegar will spoil much cream. Do not speak harshly and coldly after doing a kindness. A clap of thunder will curdle milk, and nothing will ever make it sweet again. Do not ask for favors till you have earned them or can give security that you will do so. If you have a friend, stick to him. If you owe a man, do not wait to be dunned, but settle as though it were the pleasure it should be, and is, to honest men. If in business, do not wait to settle till there will be a balance coming to you; others may need money more than you. Be a little more prompt than your word. If you are to pay a man, do it before night, as night is the next day. If you are in hard luck, never whine; never give up and let the battle go on without you. Get up and work the harder. The contents of a letter are not generally known until it is opened. Do not wear a sour face. People are afraid of such, and well they may be. If you are laboring for another, do by him as you would by yourself, only a little more so. If others are laboring for you, take an interest in them. The ivy was not intended to support the oak. Men do not like to work for nothing. Never promise an apple when you cannot give even a seed.

And another thing, my boy. Do not be in haste to quit. Many a girl would have said "Yes!" in another minute; many a nut would have cracked had you hit it once more. Many a tough stick of wood have we split by "one more blow." Many a mark has been hit by one more shot. Many a dollar has been collected by going for it once more. Many a fast friend has been made by one more kind word. Many a tear has been stopped by one more fond kiss. Many a home has been made happy by the spending therein one more hour each night with the loved one or ones awaiting your coming. Do not be in too great a hurry, Valter, my boy. If young, you can wait; if old, haste may take you hence too quick. Wait on others, then take your time. The river grows larger the farther it runs, and love grows stronger the longer it waits. There are years to come after this. If not, little matter who is ahead now. Do your duty, my boy. Keep your own heart ready for the race, or ready to go HOME. Deal honorably with all. Do not have too many confidants. A secret which requires two or more to hold it, is the very devil once it breaks loose.

A little word in kindness spoken, a pleasant greeting, often makes a friend who lasts for life. When the heart is light, a cold word makes it sick. When weary with care and trouble, a kind word or some trifling act sheds God's own sunshine in it. Most people have good memories. They forget a kindness, but seldom forget an injury or unkind word. A quail alights, you can see where—but who can tell where it will rise? So with kind words or cruel ones. If you cannot do a person a favor, tell him so frankly, and in such a way that he will not have ground for offence. If you cannot help a man, never promise him. Then he knows where to find you, and has respect for you. And above all, never be too stingy to be honest. When a liberal man dies, people are sorry; when a miser goes hence, people are indifferent.

The way to success is easy enough, if we only look sharp to the future and despise not the small things of life. And these small things, my boy, make the muckle for all of us.

CHAPTER VII.

SATURDAY NIGHT.

ONE by one the days go out. Saturday night comes.

One by one the hopes go out. Eternity comes. Like hailstones the days drop from the clouds of time, to fall cold and dreary into the fathomless past. Each day is a life—is a history. The hopes of the morning are tears by night—the air-castles of Monday are the graves of Saturday night, alas, too oft! God gives us sun, life, rain, health, friends, and that which is more blessed than all, golden Hope. All the rest desert us; but Hope, twin sister of Immortality, is ours through the week—into and beyond Saturday night—into the grave, to bear us dry and happy through the Stygian flood and on to God. Blessed be Hope, and blessed be the nights which call us to kneel at her altar. Changes have come during the interim between this and last Saturday night. Many a mound in the church-yard or cemetery marks God's bruises on the desolate human heart. Many a heart-joy has been dipped in sadness. Many a dress which one week since was white is now of the deepest mourning. Some mourn. Some wear mourning while the heart rejoices. Some there are whose hearts are darker than the grave, for the lamp of love is broken, and the joy of years has gone home. Scarlet buds and sombre blossoms. Such is life.

Who of us all are nearer heaven than one week since? Who of us have laid up treasures above? Who of us have mellowed the earth in which all must rest? The account is for or against us! We all thought and vowed one week since to do right, but alas for temptation! All of us have argued with the subtle reasoner—few of us have come off victorious. Prayers have been uttered since last Saturday night. Curses have been invoked. The record has been perfectly kept, and some day it will be opened to our eyes. Let us rest from labor and renew our vows. By the family fireside—by the family altar—by the cot and the couch there is much to do this night. Look back down the dark lane. See what wrecks are there strewn. Hopes which have died. Promises badly broken. Good intentions and noble resolutions lie bleeding and torn as far back as the eye can reach. Hard words lie where soft ones would have been better. There are disappointments and betrayals, bitter words and wicked acts strewn thick over the ground. Ruins—ruins—ruins! Here and there a fragrant flower lifts its silent voice and rears its pearly leaf to gladden the débris around. Here and there a blossom—here and there, but too far apart, can be seen the beautiful in strange contrast with the ruins and wrecks. Life is a dark lane. Would to God there were more flowers and fewer ruins! Would there were more loves and fewer hates. More white and less red.

How the changes come over us! What gave joy is now a pile of ashes! The lips we loved to kiss a week since, now have no nectar! The hand which once thrilled in rapture at the slight touch of love, now forgets to answer back! The eye has grown cold or worse than indifferent! Who is to blame? Some one. And why? None but God can tell truly! As the sun goes down and the Sabbath rises, let us strive again! Mother! clasp still closer to your heart the pledge you now caress, for God may want it back before another Saturday night is yours. The pet you kissed and caressed one week ago, has been taken away—who will go next! Deal gently with those who have erred. Heaven is forgiving. God is love. Strive to be happy. Let kind words, good wishes, and liberality of sentiment, expand all our hearts this night, for they are blessed influences—none too plenty.

If you have a friend, draw him closer to your heart. If you have a life in your keeping, do by it as you would be done by Pause ere you do evil. Think of the reward there is for those who resist temptation — for those who love. Look back. Listen! A little, prattling voice, now stilled in death!—a mother's gentle tones, perhaps well-nigh forgotten!—a sister's plaintive eye is calling you to happiness! Look over the past—the blessed memories—the mementos of the heart—and tell us if you are not glad that heaven is nearer by one more SATURDAY NIGHT.

CHAPTER VIII.

IN WHICH EASY LESSONS ARE GIVEN OUT.

THERE are a thousand things yet to learn, my boy. Life is a school, and most of us study on hard benches till the final dismissal comes, learning but to forget. One lesson is this, Valter. Learn to be a man—not a sneak. Do not be a counterfeit of somebody who is but a chapter of baseness. Hold your head high. No matter if your spoon be of horn instead of gold—your stockings wool instead of silk—your shoes of wood instead of leather. Strive to be a man. Do as you agree to, or give a truthful reason. Man was never made to fear his fellow. GOD is the only one outside your own heart to whom you must render a balance sheet with your winding one. If you promise, keep faith. If you pledge, by all means fulfil. Never go about the streets as a sheep cur sneaks home toward morning. Be a man. Give your reason. Take no one's footings, but run up the column for yourself. If you wish a favor, Valter, my boy, ask for it like a man, frankly and honestly. Do not whine, and dodge, and chip around the edges, but go straight to the centre at once. If you have aught against a man, out with it. Never stab in the dark—do not crawl from bud to blossom—from blossom to fruit of life, like a snake in the grass, making others shudder at your approach and leaving a track of slimy scandal to mark your route to death. Form an opinion. A wrong one is better than none, for it can be changed. Learn to rely on your own ideas. Learn to think and act for yourself, as though you were born to give and others to follow advice. Always shake a rattle-box before purchasing, and study the sense of an idea before you fall in with it. Many a deep chasm is bridged by the thinnest and rottenest of planks. Always keep something back. A nest-egg answers a twofold purpose. Never tell all you know at once. Do not squander all your earnings, my boy, for paupers are never buried in beds of roses.

When all is still—after night has pinned with golden studs her curtain of beauty, pause and think. Look well to the road you have already passed—look close to the road and its different branches as it appears before you. In the great walk of life few men retrace their steps, as the journey is tedious, and the road full of scoffers. Be very certain you are in the right one, my boy. Success is a thorny path. Its points and brambles were left on purpose to deter those who are not brave from continued skirmishes with fortune's pickets. None but men of pluck deserve success, as "none but the brave deserve the fair." Boy or man, strive for the golden future. Earn and enjoy. It *is* all of life to live, but it is not all of death to die. Look into your own heart when all is still. Look over accounts carefully and see who is getting the most credit —you or the devil. Strike out all the bad thoughts which climb over the heart-wall and take root within. Plant anew the little seeds of love and noble-hearted kindness which shed a perfume around the dying bed and make a grateful shade in which to have the final struggle with death. Never do in the night what you would be ashamed of in the daytime. Do not go ahead with your lips and hold back with your heart. Speak the truth, Valter. Who are you afraid of? Learn to be a man among men, and to be a man of honor. Such men never want for friends. Look about you. Take warning from others. There are lessons for the eye as well as for the ear. See how many scores there are whose heads are as large—whose foreheads are as high—whose eyes are as far apart as your own, but who wrecked on their own actions years since, and are fast breaking to pieces with no one to lend a hand to save. It takes but a little to lose a reputation. It takes years to acquire a good one. When you see a mean act, set it up as a finger-post. Shun it. When you see or hear of a good, a noble deed, emulate it. If not on a large scale, do it on a small one. The widow's mite was more precious than gold from the rich. When you see a man doing well in business, take lessons from him. Stick to your friends. Never throw off one of them. They are worse than broken stones to walk over when once wronged. Fish with a long pole, my boy. Throw boldly into the stream, and throw beyond your fellows. Deep water holds the larger fish. Form a purpose. Make up your mind to be *something*. If you cannot sing a song, tell a story or make a fire. If you cannot drive the horses, you can give them water; if you cannot paint a coach, you can grease an axle. If you cannot hatch chickens, you can at least put the eggs in the nest.

And never fret. Take things coolly. Do not get mad at the very moment of all others when you should hold your temper. Do not be in too great a hurry. Judgment-Day will not be till your name is called and you answer to it. Did you ever think of that? No matter of how little importance or how indefinite you are, the show will not be opened until you are duly cared for and seated. Green fruit makes people sick. Ill-gotten gains are green fruit. Never bite at the bare hook. Do not jump into all sorts of traps, dead falls, and snatch-holes, merely to please some one who delights in torture. Never go in bathing merely to give some shore-walker a chance to steal your clothes. Do not make love to a girl just to hear her sigh as she lays her head against your watch-pocket. Don't kiss babies merely to please the mother; nor would it be advisable, Valter, to kiss the mother to please the baby, for the husband might be looking from around some corner. There are several things you should not do. Do not believe that keeping a canary makes of a woman a lady. Do not believe that every girl who smiles on you is in love with you. Girls smile on a fellow as roosters crow—because others do. Do not be in too great haste to marry. Thin ice never keeps. A few years of happiness is better than several years of misery. Do not give to every one who asks. Some men, like rat-traps—never give back. Don't make up your mind that you know everything, for there is much of value not yet winnowed from the chaff of passing events. But keep your eyes open and the point of your gun well up. Better shoot over than under. Better a curve than a slant.

CHAPTER IX.

THE EVENING STAR.

HERE, by the blazing fire, while the bitter cold wind goes howling, shrieking by, is room for many a friend I could name, who never will sit around on the wide hearth as of yore. I have been out in the wind and cold five hours — five short hours — sleigh-riding. The flecks on the jet-black coat of my horse, the long frosted whiskers he sported, the creaking of the snow, the deserted look of the farm-houses we passed, the haste with which kind hands opened the door on returning, tell me it is cold without; but I did not feel it. Two of us were out riding.

A fast horse, warm plank for the feet, warm robes, merry bells, warm hearts, handsome cutter, and smooth road never yet froze a man in five hours, nor do I believe they ever will.

We went out into the country by the old church, the little school-house, the old cider-mill, the country store and the post-office, the smithy's shop, and into the broad yard where often we have driven out and in. Fifteen years since we rode out from that wide-opening gate, and, if you like, I will tell you of that ride.

It was a clear moonlight night — clear and cold. There was a party of us. We had no bells other than the rustic *belles*, whose beauty has never been surpassed. We had no superabundance of wolf-skin robes — we had no light-running cutter or extra-fast horse, as to-day; but we had six warm hearts. Oh! it was fun —sleigh-riding in those days! A long sleigh-box on two bobs, straw enough to make the hearts of half-a-dozen poor families glad—and

down in there we all sat. There were boys and
girls fifteen years since—now there are young
men and young ladies. How cosily we nestled
together in that old sleigh! How cosily each
boy's arm encircled *one*. How the heart shot
out its feelers to clasp itself around and protect
that *one*—loved more than others. How the
heart warms, expands, and rises into the throat
now as that old picture is called up! Away we
went! Some one said as we started, "Be careful, boys, and don't upset," but little heed was
paid to the caution. How cold the night was
fifteen years since! Perhaps you remember it—
it seems as if *you must* remember. Nestled together in that good old sleigh, how we glided
over the beaten track, and how our hearts glided
into *another* beaten track! Then, when the cheeks
of those we loved grew cold, we used to warm
them—no matter how. Then, fifteen years since,
lest others would hear the kindly spoken thanks,
we took them from the lips of the speaker, and

closer drew the loved form. It was cold, but we felt it not! On by the same houses as to-day we sped, and on sped our hearts, linking each to the other. How we laughed, as a sudden jolt would throw us all together! How we laughed as the foot-balls came pelting our faces, and drew the hoods together and looked in to see if *any one was hurt!* It was fifteen years ago that sleigh-rides were worth taking, but that day has gone by. Then the snow was deeper — the roads smoother —the horses faster—the girls prettier—the boys better—and the nights shorter—than now.

Then we rode up to the little grave-yard, where a few brown stones—no marble in those days—marked the last resting-places of those who had gone before us. We rode past the old church, where the congregation used to join in songs of praise. We stopped and talked among ourselves —six of us—who should first go into that yard never to return. Still closer were the loved ones drawn, and still warmer beat the hearts beneath our *homespun suit of gray*. We had laughed and talked on the way out, fifteen years ago, and as the team stood there by that silent grave-yard, and a light cloud drifted over the moon, so did a cloud drift over our hearts.

*　*　*　*　*　*

A year after that time, another party visited the little grave-yard. One of the six was *going home*. The sun shone forth coldly, as does the affection of some we call friends—to mock the scene. We went slower, fourteen years ago, than we did fifteen, but there were more of us. One of the six was riding alone, and no warm cheek could drive the cold from hers. The road was as smooth, but we drove more carefully. We passed the church without stopping—on to the little yard beyond. An open gate—a dark spot beyond—a silent gathering about a grave—tears and sobs—a prayer—uncovered heads—a lowering of one of the six where no one could take the wishes of her heart from lips closed forever—a dull, heavy, rattling sound—a benediction—a return.

* * * * * *

Fourteen years since, we drove home on that road slower than to-day — and fourteen years since, as night came on before home was reached a star arose in the east. Then I knew the soul of one I loved had gone home to God, and as pure a pearl as the sun ever saw had been set in a glorious crown.

The sun has set many times since, but that star has never gone down. The sun has set in coldness—in warmth—in most glorious splendor—and even shut itself out from us for days together; but I always see that star, and it is always the same as was the soul of her who felt no more fear, when called *home*, than when riding in that old family sleigh fifteen years since.

* * * * * *

Still there! I have been out to look upon

it, and now, as fifteen years since, that star is just above the hill, as bright as ever—and the church is the same—and the old preacher the same—and the night the same—and the sky the same—and my heart the same, but too sad to write more.

CHAPTER X.

In which Disappointment is Favorably Mentioned.

THEY went out in darkness, Valter. And life is often thus.

"Who went out in darkness?"

The sparks, my boy. Standing on the hurricane deck, we saw from the tall chimneys, thousands of golden, living, warm, and earnest sparks leaving the dark mouths of those huge iron lungs, and joyously riding the breeze. They came into the world as man comes—they rode to their eternity just which way the breeze drove them, as man rides,—each by itself. From the clear and calm depths of the water over which we glided, there came a counterpart—a wife for every spark wafted off from above us. Mirrored in its glassy surface—seeming as they floated to be romping children of the stars; up from the deep reflection came the golden shadows. Borne down by their own weight, to meet their brides, sank the burning sparks—closer and closer—nearer and yet nearer came substance and shadow—the real and the ideal. They met as lovers meet, midway 'twixt heaven's reflection and heaven itself—a kiss—a low, speaking kiss —a wedding of LIFE with HOPE—and into the dark water; borne on to a common eternity; a *cinder* floated—the spark was dead, and the swift-darting reflection was gone forever. And, my boy, as the spark wedded on the "river of death" and died, so do we all. We float, as it were, idly over the terrible reality—some reflection of our own heart meets us—an intervalic kiss—a wedding even in death, and lifeless float loved and loving on to the broad Hereafter. Stand on the

"Many a loved child has divided its sweet kiss—half to the earnest mother who brought it here from God—half to the waiting angel who took it HOME."—*Page* 79.

steamer's deck at midnight, my boy, and see the breeze-riding sparks wed their golden reflections in disappointment. Watch one darting shadow—learn a lesson.

So do you and us, Valter. The rose of anticipation often rests at last in the ashes of sad reality. Disappointment is our common lot. Many an egg fails to mother a bird. Many a flower dies while yet a bud, as promising as the plump form of youth. Full many a golden cloud has drifted into the dark homes of unborn storms and disappeared as do the castles of dreamers. Many a loved child has divided its sweet kiss—half to the earnest mother who brought it here from GOD—half to the waiting angel who took it HOME to a heaven of joy, there in the spirit-land to wait and bless with the fruition of angelic love the tired heart it fled from—to dry forever the tearful eyes of maternal fondness. From the coffin of disappointment often rise golden realizations, as beautiful butterflies are born of ugly caterpillars.

Disappointment Favorably Mentioned.

Many a man has before now dived deep into the sea of business or matrimonial life, but no pearls rewarded his dangerous risk. Hearts have wedded shadows—have wedded icebergs—have wedded sorrow—have wedded anguish; the children of each being disappointment. Millions of meteors flash athwart the distant sky, and leave but space. Many a man is by Time shot into Eternity, the target of life not penetrated in its remotest corner. Thousands of flowers are crushed under the foot of man and die alone. It is disappointment—but *next season*, the life-holding root sends into the world a bud which blossoms with such fragrance that invisible spirits protect it. The disappointment of last year is the blessing of the present. The soul of the plant turned back to renewed effort and richer rewards, and the pearly blossoms came again to deck the bride or vigil the corpse.

This world is full of disappointments, my boy; and it is overflowing with stern realities. Wishes are born in our hearts and their children beget disappointments as the wind begets moans. Some are for good — some evil. Time alone can tell. Go back on memoric paths, and see how often disappointment has brought disappointment! Many a time has the heart of childhood wept over sorrow which proved the chrysalis of happiness. Many a tear-wet pillow at night has been the resting-place of joy in the morning. Many a cavern of sadness has been the antechamber to happiness richer than dreams ever brought us, Valter. Many a fit of sickness has been the renewing of Life's great policy, and from many a grave has there gone into the world again, a freed and loving heart, trembling within its own silence with the sight of some distant dove bringing a new lease of life — a chapter of joys, with sorrows and repinings omitted. Many a cold wind has blown away the heart miasma, though its blasts piped right merrily for a time, and we trembled at the storm which brought us the sun. We are all born to trouble, Valter, my boy. In every heart is a safe—GOD knows where the key is. In every heart is some secret of life or death. In the life of every man, morn, noon, and night are marked with disappointment. It is the grave of events from which spring and grow vigorous deeds. Peace follows war, as shadows follow the sun. The thicker the ice, the deeper must have been the water. The longer lasts the winter, the more rapidly comes the sun which starts anew the frozen current. Disappointments are the lessons of life. They are its dark backgrounds which set forth the most lasting and beautiful pictures. Life is a forest. In it, are dead trees and living ones. The one give shade—let us rest under their protecting branches. Sorrow makes the heart better. Disappointments renew our love. The impeded river stops not forever, but finds a new current, and like the flashing of His anger, rushes on with new force. What if you have been disappointed? Others have been. All may look cold to-day—it will not so look to-morrow. Often, my boy, the deepest sorrows have brought the choicest blessings — the sickness of Hope proved the convalescence of Joy. Many a ghost has proved a shadow—many a dreaded lake, the suspended mirage—many a mountain but a bank of fog. Do not sit in the cold, my boy. Rest only where happiness or success is beside you. The grave is but the reception-room to heaven, dreary though it seem. Life often ends in disappointment, but it can end in happiness. Do not stop to regret the past. Let the dead bury the dead—look ahead—to future scenes. Sorrow is sent to make us purer—trouble to make us better —disappointment to increase our bravery. Never give up. NEVER SAY FAIL! Never be discouraged. Failure is the servant and success the child of effort. Look up. Look to the future—of this life; of the coming one. Your heart may be the cemetery of a thousand disappointments—

there is room yet for leafy-boughed success to spring from and around every grave; making the blessed future a labyrinth of bowers—a wilderness of joy—an ocean of prosperity—a heaven of heartfelt bliss.

CHAPTER XI.

Wherein-Common-Sense is Entitative.

"WALTER, my boy, it is a good thing there are none.

"None—what?"

Windows to the heart, my boy. Little do we know what prompts man to action. The grass comes nodding and kissing—now bent low with tears—then standing proudly erect—carpeting the earth with loveliness. The tiny sprouts are much like the human heart. Each blade has its own mission—its own dewy tears to shake off—its own handsome green to make itself beautiful. When one shoot is cut down, another one springs forth—in time, and no other blade waits its growth. It is so, my boy, with the human heart. None of us know why one is happy and another miserable. It is well we do not. It is a good thing we have no windows, for then we should be so busy looking in upon the secrets and sorrows of others, that our own would be opened to the world, as the clouds are thrown out in relief by the glorious sunset. We all have aims. All have motives. All have causes for joy—for tears—for smiles—for sobs—for hopes—for actions. What if the causes are not published —none the less do they exist.

There is not a heart, my boy, but has its inner chamber, the key of which has been given to God. There is not a heart but has its grave of hopes, although the foliage of time may have hidden it from the world, and almost from our own sight. Many a one you and we condemn God pities—many we pity He condemns. Let us have common sense, my boy, and attend to our own matters. No one cares for another's trouble. The only headache we are sorry for, is the one on our own shoulders. The only wound we really care for, is that which pains our mother's child. People never care for other people. As boys whistle when passing a grave-yard in the night, so do men talk of others to hide their own troubles. It is true, my boy, that when you and we do well, others are jealous, or envious.

Be liberal, my boy. If not with money, with kindness. Little do you know why the heart of yonder man is sad. God knows, and that will do. People will seldom inquire into another's troubles, with good motives. The world hunts for sorrows as boys hunt the garret for balls to knock about and see them bound. If you have a ball and do not wish it knocked—keep it out of sight. That, Valter, my boy, is true philosophy. If you have trouble—fight it. If you don't kill it, it will kill you. Life is short. Be a man, and leave the rest to futurity. Praise that which is good. None of us are perfect. What one does to-day another does to-morrow. Had you been in his or her place, you might, my boy, have done even worse.

The world moves by day as well as by night. It moves while we are happy and while we are miserable, just the same. Let us have common-sense enough to be happy while we can, and not bother our heads or hearts with that which concerns us not except to do good. Give an opinion when it is asked. This world is badly mixed, my boy. When so many come rushing in to see the show or hear the concert, even "reserved seats" contain queer crowds. Tickets get mixed. People are huddled together regardless of propriety, and many are glad when the show is out. If all the big and little people in the world could be hived, and when they thought no one was looking, you and we could peep in and see—what a sight! If all our hearts were to be opened at noon, many a suicide would be chronicled at half-past eleven—many a one would change his name at half-past twelve. Go slow, my boy. Do not form an opinion as you would fall out of bed. If a bridge carries you safe over, it is a good one. If it lets you fall through, do not lose time in cursing it, but try another. If riding in the cars be dangerous and you cannot take the risk, go afoot. If the wagon rides roughly, jump out and walk. If riding in a ship makes you sea-sick, stay at home. If a friend did not treat you well the first time you called, you are a very foolish Valter, my boy, to visit him again. If tobacco makes you sick, eject it, and do not give others spasms by making wry faces. If the coat does not fit you, get one that will, or go without. Do not fret, and bother, and worry, and stew, and grumble, and find fault, and haggle, and whine over your hard luck, but go in your shirt-sleeves. If the weather be cold, exercise. If it be warm, who wants a coat?

Don't be inquiring into other people's affairs

at all—much less when you have affairs of your own. If you have business, attend to it. If you have none, the business of others should not concern you. If you cannot take a trick, throw up your hand—if fish will not bite, look for another stream, or quit that kind of sport.

CHAPTER XII.

IN WHICH WE SPEAK ABOUT PLUCK.

WALTER, my boy, what do you consider as God's best gift to man?

"Woman, of course."

Well—that is very good; but as woman is never *given* to man without his *winning* her, there is something else.

"Money?"

No, my boy—the root of evil is hardly a good gift, as it is the source of more misery and trouble than happiness.

"Good looks?"

Wrong again, my boy. Good looks, as the

world speaks, fade, wither, and die. Handsome infants seldom make handsome adults—time works too many changes. The inner beauty of the soul which shines and radiates as trouble and sorrow gather around the heart, is seldom seen by the world. But there is a gift which is always noticed. And that bestowment is Pluck. Give us that, and all else follows. With a brave heart none need fail. What if you fall once, twice, twenty, or a hundred times? Pluck will pick you up, and each time nerve your heart for a greater effort. Life is a succession of hills and valleys. They rise before us, my boy, in all matters of existence. In love, wealth, ambition, success or power, it is up here—down yonder. Look around and see for yourself who it is that succeeds. Not the timid one, who at sight of the first obstacle in his path loses heart and yields the game. Not the man whose nerve will not keep his upper lip and under jaw in place. Not the man who gives up on the first trial. These men do not succeed. Success often sports with a man as a shy trout plays with the hook of the angler. Keep cool—be steady—stick to a regular business, and soon the nibble will end in a snapping bite, and you will land the wary prize safely at your feet.

Pluck will do anything, my boy. It will win the girl you love. Not in itself, perhaps, but it will give you the qualities she admires. Women seldom wed men—they wed ideas. Pluck will fill your pockets with gold—but that is not the object of life. It will carve your way to eminence, and encircle you with friends who will pile the sod over your grave in sorrow—the heartfelt sigh, telling, in eloquence beyond expression, the love they bore you. Keep a stiff upper lip, my boy. Failure is the rule—success the exception. A million men walk boldly up to the great object of life—and then have not the courage to take hold of it. A million others fail because the way seems so long—or the road is too rough

Others fail for *fear* they will not succeed. This life is a school, my boy. There are many lessons to learn. We have each a thousand objects—nine hundred too many—and flit from one to another, as the humming-bird dashes from bud to flower—and life is all frittered away before we know it. Have a purpose. Take aim. Shoot at something. Make a mark, if nothing but a dent in the mud. If you cannot run up the hill, climb it. If you cannot reach the top, go as high as possible—then pass just one man more. If you die—die game. If you sink, let it be in deep water. If you reach for a flower, take the best one. If you fail—get up like a man and try again. Children cry and whimper—leave off tears when you vote.

The road may be rough, my boy, but whoever was made in the image of God should never say any road was too rough. Brambles may beset your path—make for the centre, as the hardest-pointed ones are those on picket duty. If you lack perseverance, have pluck to cultivate it. If you lack money, have pluck to earn it. If you lack credit, have pluck to be honest and to show people that you deserve confidence. If you lack position, have pluck to begin at the bottom of the hill and work up. The apex is broad enough for all who have the daring to struggle upward to it—and so distant that few ever reach it. If you lack decision of character, have pluck enough to keep away from temptation. If you have no umbrella, do not stand around in the rain. If the monosyllable "no" is a good word to use—have pluck to speak it plain and distinct. Never choose the road that is the shortest, if the other one is better. Never fail to satisfy your own heart—others will be satisfied in time.

Straw men are never fit for anything except to fool crows from a cornfield. The men who build railroads, steamboats, factories, and cities, are never cowards. The man who succeeds in anything, is he who has pluck. And that little word, my boy, has a powerful meaning. It signifies something more than bull-dogism, and you can study it out at leisure. Never despair. A thousand dark and rainy mornings have ended in the most glorious sunsets. Many an almost impenetrable swamp has but stood sentry to a golden land beyond. Many a cloud has passed over, and left behind it a clear sky. Many a cannon has been fired without a ball in it. Many a mountain has proved but a mirage. Have a heart for every fate. If in hard luck—it might be harder. And then Valter, my boy, you will succeed. Pluck is the genii whose resources are limitless—whose power is magic. Pluck first—luck afterward. With the first, all else will follow.

CHAPTER XIII.

KNITTING.

TO-DAY, I have been looking at a knitting-machine. It is a marvellous invention—able to knit a stocking in four minutes! I don't like it. It is an infringement, and should not be tolerated. Years ago, before gray hairs began to show themselves on my head, there was another knitting-machine I loved to watch. I can look back the narrow lane of life and see it now. I can see an old brown house, surrounded by fruit-trees and lilacs. I can see in it, by the old-fashioned hearth, which was warmer then than now—even like the hearts of men—a fair and good woman. I can see her sitting there of a winter night, by the light of a pine knot, winding yarn from the ball, and shaping it into stockings, as we wind yarn from the ball of life, and shape it into good or bad fitting actions. Her needles used to click, click, click, as regular as the beatings of a heart close by, beside of mine, in another room. They were happy days then. Life looked brighter then than now. Her knitting was even as was her life; and warmer than the lamb's-wool stockings she knit, was the heart that smiled—when to others that were poor she gave. I used to sit in the adjoining room, Saturday nights, and sit there hours after the good old lady had put up her knitting for the night. Another sat beside me. We listened to the click of the needles, to the beating of our hearts, to the chirp of a cricket— apt cricket—on the hearth; and later in the evening, to the whistle of the whippoorwill in the grove below. We were knitting. We gazed forth on nature, and talked of the present. We sat hand in hand, and looked at the stars and the future, and wondered why people were not always happy. Earlier in the evening, before the good old lady had quit work, softly indeed must be the kiss, gently sealed on the pure brow of her beside us, that she did not hear. We were all happy then but her. Now in heaven she is at rest, while the occupants of the parlor in those days are longing for different and whiter yarn to knit from than they have.

A marble slab—plain like his life, erect as was his walk—overshadowed by a close-limbed willow—as was his life by good deeds—its leaves beating back the burning rays of the sun—as his good actions had ever beat back calumny—marked well the little spot in the garden, more loved by the knitter than all other spots. Years before, a warm heart beat in unison with her own. Loving kisses were gently offered upon her brow to the shrine of love and goodness, but now she stood in the front of her battle, alone. Once in a while would she drop a stitch, but oftener would she drop a tear, and the lip would quiver as if shaken by the winds of the past. At such times would I narrow, and knit the threads of life closer; and yet closer would I draw that other heart to mine, wishing that some day my grave might be wet with as sacred dew as was the one in the garden. At times would the old lady unravel several rounds from her stocking, and at times would she unravel several years from her work of life, and strewing them about her feet, look them over, and then on bended knee gather them up, and offer them to the inspection of HIM, above. Her work was approved; and as she came in to say "goodnight," I know of two hearts that grew larger and warmer. But one day she lingered too long by the grave—the April air was too chill; and well was it that the visit was a long one, as it was her last BUT ONE. When the heart is warm cold winds, or cold actions either, strike it the more severe, and the cold wind struck her. She gave up her knitting; the ball of yarn and of life were both used up at once, and her needles were laid away simultaneously with her *last* visit to the weeping willow. Always would her ball unwind clear to the centre—yarn all the way—no wad of paper, or chip, or walnut was used to start it over. So with her life. No black spot was found in the centre after she was gone; and not greener grows the willow to-day than is the memory of that good woman.

Time flew slower then than now. A stocking was not made in four minutes, as to-day. Hearts were not as deeply located then as at present. Life had more of sweet, and less of bitter, though a bitter draught came; and a score of years have not taken from me the taste. Another form was laid under the willow; and all the bright spots I had looked upon in the future, vanished, never to return. I would like to step back to those days, but 'tis better to hasten on. The spirit-world is large, and some one is ever waiting, inside the golden gate, for the loved and left. I don't like knitting. I don't like to see stockings turned off by machinery the same as persons live and love.

CHAPTER XIV.

WE WALK IN THE COLD, AND PITY WHERE OTHERS CONDEMN.

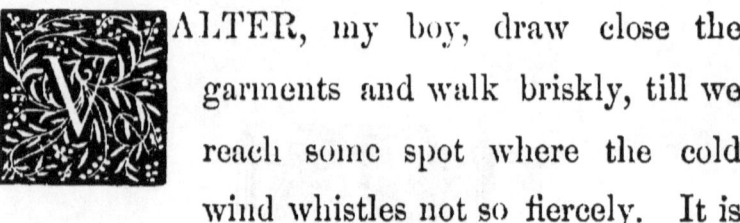

WALTER, my boy, draw close the garments and walk briskly, till we reach some spot where the cold wind whistles not so fiercely. It is a cold—yes, a bitter cold morning. The smoke hates to leave warm chimneys, and, my boy, you will see that it actually refuses to leave where there is no fire—waiting to be warmed! The little snow-birds sit on fences, and look puffy-like, as does a narrow-souled man sporting a military uniform. How the foot wakens the sleeping frost-king, and creaks with crispness every time the quick-stepping foot rests on the crumbling snow! On the windows of all the houses, the workmen of Zero have worked with subtle fingers, and left their delicate tracings. Ah! my boy, how feeble is man—how ignorant—how weak! It is cold, my boy, very cold.

Did you ever stop to realize how little love there is in this great world of ours? People never care for others half as much as they pretend to. Even in summer they are very cold, with blood at fever heat. Their hearts will freeze spirits! We have a few friends, but never love them half as much as we ought, or profess to. When we pick the berries from a bush, how quick we leave it! Perhaps the warm sun and blessed light may ripen other berries there, and then how we scramble for them, no matter what other beautiful shrubs, prettily growing, are trampled to death! People are too selfish—too cold. Yet such is nature; and there is, perhaps, but little use in warring against it.

Now Valter, my boy, did you ever notice how soon some people will leave their best friends when in trouble? And how they will slander, abuse, and libel the unfortunate, lest some one should think they were once friends? If a man fails in business, through misfortune, how people shun him! If a strong man is tempted more than he can bear, and falls, how few friends who will encourage him to rise again! Society is a queer god. It is a very hollow, deceitful thing. Yet we all follow its dictation, as slaves follow a master they both dread and despise. If a girl falls, how her sex—her angelic sex even—desert her, and let hunger, disease, and death take her hence, unwept and uncared for save by those who are like her, carrying the hell of wanton dissipation forever within their cruelly wronged hearts. No matter how dearly we once professed to love, too often the least breath of trouble will drive us all from where once was happiness, and the heart will grow, oh! so cold! If a person is going on foot, people seldom care to be company through the journey; but if he rides in a carriage better than our own, we are very willing to sit beside him.

"Don't like such friends!"

Well, Valter, my boy, such are too often the only friends we have. Few are the hearts which will stand the pressure of misfortune. Few are the friends who will stick like a brother till life has gone hence—few are the hearts which sympathize with the sorrow of those they once professed to—perhaps did—love. Few are the men or women who cannot be bought away, or bribed away from those they once said they would share the last dollar with, or, if called upon, to lay down life for. Once in a while, such a person is found. We know those whom trial only strengthens, whom trouble only helps, whom sorrow only makes more loving—more willing—more generous — more noble — more kind and good. But there are few, and only those whose hearts have suffered more cruel pangs than the world knew of—whose life had become darkened —whose heart, long lost, had at last been found by one who could love, cherish, and, without jealousy or mistrust, appreciate the love it gave, the sacredness of its devotion—the strength of its purpose, and who would know how true it beat in unison with kindred feeling.

The style of the world, my boy, is to hitch on to those who are going up—to cut loose from those going down. It is fashionable to desert persons when misfortune has overtaken them— when *others* are deserting them, even without cause—to hit the under man in the fight. If trouble, sorrow, remorse, or affliction have sobered a man's face, or dressed him in coarser clothes, everybody shuns him, because a cold, heartless, hollow, unfeeling world claps its hands and urges on the chase. Yes, my boy, there is more in this world that is cold than the weather.

In heaven, they say, everybody loves. Not

as the bridegroom loves his bride—as the warm-hearted girl whose eyes are deeper than the azure of heaven—whose heart is wrapt up in, and lives only for one she worships—not as the libertine loves—not as the depraved and unfeeling love, but as the infant loves the mother on whose heart its delicate ear listens for the counter-ticking of its own life—as we love the good and noble here below. Valter, my boy, that is a blessed Hope then. Even if eternity is to be devoted to labor, it will be too short, if love be the reward. And, my boy, how great and wondrous the change before many are fit to enter there! Many Christians, as they call themselves, are not prepared for such bliss. They may profess before men — may deceive some with their long faces, but they are too cold to ever know the happiness in store for those whose hearts are ever warm and generous. Biting frost is disagreeable, my boy, but there is something colder. We may feel cold toward some — who can help destiny? The severest frost is that of the heart, and how desolate the blight where hope has fled — where love has gone! Yet, my boy, there is happiness in learning who are false — who are true friends. Butterflies leave the jessamine when its flowers begin to fall, but the little wren builds her nest underneath, and beneath its shelter rears her young, nor leaves it until ready for another home far away.

CHAPTER XV.

Wherein the Use of Eyes is Looked Over.

WALTER, my boy, the road we are travelling day after day, to and from our regular place of business, is one so well known that a blind man could walk it—if he only knew all the crooks, turns, broken planks, holes, and dangers therein. But there is another road, my boy, to walk safely over which needs eyes. Not dead eyes, covered by carelessness as plants are covered by newspapers and other sheets to guard them against frost, but live eyes, which register as fast as the impression is received. There is the physical walk through life and the spiritual walk to eternity. Not one man in twenty knows what his eyes were made for. Optics are like trotting horses—the best-trained ones get over the most ground. The vision of some people points inwardly, no matter where it starts from. One man walks heedlessly along and stumbles from a steamboat. Another jumps from one car to another, and, because he could not see danger, foolishly becomes a candidate for a hearse and sextonical orders. Another man walks along the road—stubs his toe, and then picks himself up, looking very foolish and afraid some one saw his downfall. A lady with silk and satin well arranged and displayed on her fair form, is so intent on winning eyeshots from some loaferish crowd that she runs against dry-goods boxes, rubs against door jambs or awning posts, and rends her dress or daubs its smooth folds with close-sticking paint. Another person, my boy, is always late at the cars—late at church—late everywhere, because he does not see how time flies.

Eyes were given us for a wise purpose. We have two of them. That means something, my boy. And they have an outer reflection and an inner one. Your eyes are young yet. They will bear much training. Teach them what to do, my boy, and well will they perform. Not that you must speak of all they see or what they gather in. The little brain-pictures they photograph will, if preserved, make an abundant stock in trade for any person. Eyes are wealth to one who has learned his trade.

And there is much to see with the inner eye. We will walk along slow, and learn. You, Valter, my boy, may see the pictures we have saved.

The man who is always late at business never will be wealthy unless by accident. The woman who hangs invisible weights to her chin whenever talking to her husband—whose welcoming smiles are convex, with acidulated edges, never adds over-much to her store of happiness. Well trained eyes see much of this. They see wives smiling on every one, except their husbands. This is a sad picture—with more of misery for a background than the world, with all its smartness, ever sees. And, my boy, there are men whose laughs, songs, jests, and anecdotes are given liberally outside their family. Good eyes will see the reason—poor eyes will not notice— medium eyes will wonder at the fact. And there are men who go on from year to year, betraying confidence—selling friends—dishonoring trusts reposed in them—abusing the sacred ties of friendship—swindling their own hearts—blunting and wearing down the fine edges of conscience—liberally planting death or disease in their frames—retrograding from the goal of lofty ambition and honorable purpose. Their eyes only see *to-day*—to-morrow is beyond the scope of their vision. And, my boy, there are eyes of men which fall in love with small feet—with red cheeks—with a certain colored eye—with a curl or ringlet—with a style of dancing—with a machine-made smile—with a white neck or with hills of snow, summit-finished with living violets. All these things in themselves are vanities, my boy. The purchase made for one of these beauties wears like plaster-of-Paris statuary—soft, hollow—light, and certain to turn a dingy shade. Small feet may be cut off by cars or distorted with rheumatic pains. Red cheeks may thank French saucers, severe pinching, drugs, or disease, for an existence. The fancy eye, unless the heaven-born love-light burns well and steady therein, is more dreaded to look upon than a battle-field. The curl which electrified you, as it fell down upon your face, or just touched your neck by accident, may have been made by barbers' tongs, or may be driven away by fever. People do not always dance, my boy. Machine smiles are like Barlow knives—fit for children only. The white neck married by gas-light may show better in two hours after the ceremony on a colored cloth than on the beautiful veins so freshly playing under the skin below. The little hills of snow may be colder than Alpine glaciers—may disappear like articles in the hands of a magician, or friendship when adversity comes, or from causes which follow effect, and the violets thereon will become, like paper flowers, misshapen and odorless. All these single pictures, which catch the glance of surface-seeking eyes, make poor anchors to drag on, while riding out the dark hours of life.

And, Valter, my boy, there are eyes of women which look not beyond the shade of their lashes —which but glance at the column of figures without noticing the footings. And the footings of figures and the footings of life are much the same. Large or small, as set in proper places. These eyes see only a nice pair of whiskers—a soft hand—a neat instep—a curly head of hair — a gold watch and seal—a swaggering gait—

a broadcloth case full of style. And, my boy, wedlock gives good women whose greatest fault is poor eyes, to these men—as you and us for want of better places hang our coats on dead limbs, our hat on the door-knob, our watch on a gimlet bored into the wall, or throw a vest on a bunch of thistles.

We all have a long walk ahead. A very long walk, my boy, and you nor us know just when the gate will open and we shall step forth. And, my boy, light will be our dress—few the suits. And as we walk down the path which leads from the shore of the dark river, how much will we see which now escapes observation! The road walked in life will be walked again, and thousands of little things now unnoticed will stand forth like sentinels. And, my boy, you and us will wonder why our eyes never beheld their index fingers, guiding right or left. Plain will they be then. Large will grow our eyes as that new path is walked; its beauties and deformities now unnoticed, made manifest—each knoll of sorrow, or bower of happiness, marked by sighs or thrills of joy, forgotten, unnoticed, or uncared for.

As we walk down that path, the eye will drink in the whole of God's scenery thickly studded with man's actions; and the black smoke of regret will too often smother out the incense of happy memories.

Then, many a man will see where his bark of happiness was wrecked, and wonder why he did not use his eyes before. There will be millions of reefs, rocks, and shoals to be seen, over and by which we all have run. Men will see the skeletons of their hopes of happiness hanging exposed to every wind—to every remark—to every eye. They will hang on cold snow-hills—on waving curls—on diamond-girted fingers—on red cheeks—on hollow accomplishments; traps set in life by deceit, to catch victims for remorse. The wine-cup and wassail bowl will lie thick along that path, and in each will be the anchored skeleton of some manly heart—some noble soul. You and us, my boy, will then see on what hollow and worthless reeds we have leaned for support—on what cold hearts we have some time or other laid our hopes—on what uncongenial spirits we have lavished affection. We shall see, my boy, where often in life we failed—we shall see warning posts now unnoticed, but none the less there. Yes, Valter, my boy, that day will be a busy one for the eyes, and happy will be he who looks well about him here. There is so much work to do. All not done in the forenoon must be done in the afternoon. There will be new mating and unmating then; new aims and new objects, for we shall see aright.

Let you and us, my boy, no matter how others use their eyes, keep ours open while awake, and day by day learn what they were given us for.

CHAPTER XVI.

IN WHICH WE FIND SMILES AMONG TEARS, AND HAPPINESS WHERE WE HAD NOT LOOKED FOR IT.

PEOPLE never know how to be happy, my boy. There is not one of God's living images but has anchored in his heart a boat which braves out, and tosses upon life's rough sea, waiting, as it rocks and pitches, for a full freight of happiness at some future day. That is the failure, Valter. We ever look ahead for some day, when care, trouble, and sorrow shall be banished. That day will never come on earth, my boy. We may look ahead—the morrow may be golden—till the morrow comes. As we walk along this road, away from the dusty city, you and us can talk quietly over these matters. We can talk of little things unnoticed by those who are in great haste to finish this book for one they know not of.

The tree which spreads its branches out as a mother holds her hands to the tottling infant, seeming to ask us to be seated under its leaves, looks inviting, but its trunk is covered with bugs and ants. The beautiful green leaf, which toys with the evening breeze, bears on its under surface insect cities which will hasten its fall. The limb above us is half decayed, though the foliage thereon is yet green and fresh. The little white stone at our feet, is the roof for ugly worms and beetles. The rose which laughs at its escape from yonder hedge — the rose which looks so sweet, has in its centre leaves a score of little bugs. The lovely dahlia, so beautiful in its delicately tinted hues, is without fragrance. The handsome oil painting, on close examination seems like a daub, made by amateur hands. The

"* * * As a lover hangs by one hand over the banister, to kiss the lips so sweet to him."—*Page* 121.

crimson cloud seemingly hanging from heaven to kiss earth, as a lover hangs by one hand over the bannister to kiss the lips so sweet to him, are not different from the morning banks of fog, only as reflecting the sun's rays. The pearly stream singing by us is often roiled, and its bed is the home of reptiles. The finest hair of your head, my boy, is in reality like the cylinder to a thrashing-machine. The mysterious photograph, on close inspection, reveals all the imperfections on the face of the setter. The rustling silk has yawning stitches to mar its beauty. The wished-for country has its dark side—the thronged city knows more misery than pen or tongue can tell.

On everything, my boy, the destroyer has set his seal. There is nothing perfect. Still we can make the most of what we have. We can walk along through life—passing by the dark scenes—lingering to-day by those of beauty, of joy and love. If to-morrow brings others, well and good.

If not, the happiness we find to-day is clear gain. We must learn to take the bitter with the sweet. Roses grow on brambles. Flowers of beauty and fragrance spring from the most neglected places. There is joy and happiness everywhere, if we do not look for too much at a time. Some of these evenings, Valter, you and us will sit quietly down, and by ourselves have a picture of happiness. Not now, my boy, but very soon.

The morning sun is the most pleasant. Its hot, mid-day beams are not what we want. Full rays of happiness bring more misery along than we can endure. Let us be thankful for what we have, and all will be well. Enjoy the present— hope for the future. The hour may look dark— there is light beyond. Be happy while you can. When in the house, do not put your head out of the window, to see how hard the blast is piping. Keep still, and thank God you are safe for a moment—if no longer. Borrow no trouble. It will be left at your door as fast as you wish to use it.

The iceman calls in the morning, and leaves the cold crystal, in small or large cakes, as you use. Time leaves cakes, chunks, and blocks of trouble in the same way. Daily he leaves them. Ice is not colder—ice will not melt quicker, if you but leave it out of doors. If you have no use for trouble, do not go or send out for it, my boy. Let it lie and melt. *Lie* and melt is a good idea, Valter. Let it waste itself in the ground—and in time, green will be the grass, rich and varied the flowers which will spring forth to be culled by your own hands.

Every man is monarch in his own heart. In his own castle, the king can be safe—in his hut, the occupant can bar the door, and none but bidden guests can enter. So can you and us do, my boy, with the door of our hearts. Admit none but friends—shut out trouble and be happy. We get the strength of tea by steeping, so do we feel the nightmare of sorrow by brooding and worrying over trouble, either real or imaginary.

Grief seldom kills — true friends never desert you. Leeches quit when they have sucked their fill of blood. So, many friends desert you when they know your troubles. If you would ride safe, be your own driver. Never trust the reins with another. Then you can go singing on your way, and be happy. If you wish one to ride with you, ask not the first you overtake, except you know who it is. Perhaps you will wish to ride alone. Better go a thousand miles to find a friend than take in one who is not.

Look around, my boy. Look ahead to the work of life, with heart and nerve. Then all troubles vanish. Look back, and you will see a thousand incidents in life—now sacred to memory—then uncared for and almost unnoticed. They were moments of happiness studding the dome of life, as the golden-headed bolts stud the floor of God above us, and glisten in mysterious tremor while we sleep. We pass them daily, little heeding the fact, as the traveller passes parallels of the meridian—to look back and see them far in the past. We can look back and see how much we have missed in not knowing which were our happy moments—and, my boy, we can also in retrospect wonder and wonder how little troubles could have worried us so in the days or hours thereof.

The trouble is, my boy—we think every one is happier than ourselves—more comforts by the family hearth than we enjoy; while the truth is that not one in ten are as happy as ourselves, or get through the world with as little trouble. The breeze might have been a hurricane—the shower a hailstorm. The friends we at times lose were never good ones, or they would not fall off as do rose leaves, themselves worthless, while the pod with the germ of so many beautiful flowers remains. Valter, just think, now, if you are not much happier than you thought you were.

CHAPTER XVII.

A SHORT TALK ABOUT HOW TO GET ALONG.

IT always was and ever will be so. Life is the same unceasing battle to-day as it was yesterday, and, my boy, there is not the least bit of use in allowing yourself to be discouraged. The darkest hour is just before day, in business as in time.

There is always a silence, thick and oppressive, before a storm—a deathly stillness before a clap of thunder. There are times when the heart malaria sickens the whole man, and thought flies wild like a loosened kite. Every person will have blue hours. Serve them as a dog serves drops of water—shake them off. Run, walk, or crawl into the sunshine, and be happy.

It does not take much, Valter, my boy, to make a man rich. Gold will not do it. Bank stock will not do. Property stolen from the poor, ignorant, and unfortunate of earth will never bring a competency. Happiness never rides in such a carriage. Man can do anything. If you want a fortune, labor for it. If you wish influence, there is but one way to get it. If you wish to lead, show your qualities. Do not be in a hurry. Leaders never drive. He who drives is in the rear. Success may seem a long distance ahead, but labor, wrapped in perseverance, will do everything.

Look around us, Valter, my boy, and see the rich earth—the carpet He gave all His creatures to walk on—the laughing, leaping, singing brook, which lover-like kisses the lips of its guide, and runs joyously on, sparkling and dancing for joy at the good it has done. See the deep woods—listen to the sounds of happy life therein—listen to the beautiful birds as they sing of love—look at the numberless flowers, sentinels of beauty—follow the deep shadows till they are lost in your own heart—look up—*up*—UP, beyond the leafy roof, into the deep blue of heaven. Stand on the sea-shore—observe the millions of shells, once homes for wondrous life—watch the waves as they bring their white-capped offerings to your very feet—hear the sea-spirit sullenly moaning down the shore, and then THINK.

God made all these. He fashioned the perfect dome and riveted it with myriads of golden bolts. In the night you can see them. All this He made out of nothing. He was never discouraged. We are made in his image—all that he made. is given us. Then why should we fail? Do not expect to centre the mark every time. Never worry if failure dares dispute the way. The strongest guards are always before the richest cities. The most difficult locks protect the richest treasures.

Labor will win. The rose does not spring from chaos to the bosom of the bride. The ivy does not twine itself around the oak as the lightning writes its name around its shaggy sides. The modest four-o'clock, and the blushing morning-glory do not open their beauty to the world as a man opens his eyes after a hurried sleep. The golden grain does not spring from the earth as the Indian arrow flies from its tensioned bow—but, like man, takes its allotted time. The girl you love will not say "yes" as a toad catches flies, the first time you ask her to share your life and lot—the ice does not melt as powder flashes—the sun does not set as a candle drops into a well.

Take time, my boy. Don't hurry too fast. Go slow, especially till you know the road, or become acquainted with your team. Be careful. Mark the rough, dangerous places you have passed, and shun them hereafter. One feather will not break a camel's back—but it will help. It is easy to succeed if you but *will* it. Make up your mind, and persevere. Mind your own business, Valter, and then, my boy, you are happy. Don't stop to club whiffets—don't stop to retail gossip—don't stop to tell your secrets—but go on, minding your own business, leaving the question of reward, life, happiness, and heaven, with God.

And remember, Valter, my boy, that no one cares for you, on general principles. You are a good orange so long as society's children can squeeze juice out of you—no longer. People never care for your troubles—they have enough of their own. People are willing to give every one's property but their own. So with secrets. They will let yours loose, and keep theirs in the stable. And they always keep the nicest fruit for home consumption—giving the poor that which they will not use themselves. And,

Valter, my boy, that is much the way they give advice—and while you eat, they laugh at your poverty and are disgusted with your appetite.

Men sport with another's sorrows or troubles as a cat plays with a mouse—only sorry when death puts an end to the torment. Men care for you, my boy, as they care for a horse that kicks. If he lets fly, quick and sharp, they keep clear of his heels.

Remember, my boy, man is a perfect machine. He is ready for life and its duties. God made us all correct. And His machines are not the ones to fail. Keep your pluck. Hold up your nerve. If others don't care for you, you are a double-headed fool to care for them. Help yourself—light your own lamp—make your own position—shoot your own gun—look out for yourself and keep a clear conscience—be independent, then let the world howl, laugh, or whine, as it pleases.

CHAPTER XVIII.

Fireside Musings.

THERE is a great white counterpane of snow on the ground this Saturday night. God's charity, covering a multitude of sins! Would that human charity would do thus—would whiten over the little bunnocks and ridges of life which can be removed from one place only to rise again in another! The week just passed has been a short one. Too short for many a one to settle with himself, yet he has *gone home.* How time flies! Has it always passed thus rapidly? If all the Saturday nights GOD has ever given us were before us, what an array of crime would be seen! Yet the day comes when they will all loom up with their debits and credits to curse or bless. Do you ever pause to think, reader? If so, pause again. If not, begin now. Draw your chair to the fire. Turn the light so that it will not hurt your eyes. Pull the curtain down at the corners. Listen! A footstep on the creaking snow. Some laborer going to his loved ones. Weary and heart-tired—may GOD warm his little home with love! Look back over the past week. It is not far. A room with seven folding doors! Open all of them. Turn the rooms into a hall—look down its short walls and see in memory the pictures you have hung thereon. Another footstep! How the boot creaks as the snow is crunched beneath its weight! Listen! A lighter step. Some wife who is hastening home to greet her husband with the marketing for the morrow. Tired man. He sits and rests with little hands in his whiskers—little eyes peering into his—

little heads on either shoulder—stars which rank him a major-general in the service of life! Hold them closer—kiss them fondly to-night. Who but God knows which one will be in shroud, coffin, or grave ere another Saturday night comes round?

Another step! The other way! Some husband with heart full of ruined hopes going to revel at the beer table. Some foolish youth, swift stepping by, anxious to join the revel. Pitied husband. It was not thus a few years since. Who is to blame? Let us, who know not the cares and shadows of the heart, do not that which God has forbidden. Let us not condemn. He will reward and He will punish. The step dies away. Around the corner. So her hope dies away. So his heart-thoughts have died out. Why will he leave the home fireside this Saturday, over all others? Home once had charms. The eye now so indifferent, once lit its way to his very soul. The lips now cold, except in petulancy, once put their full richness up to revel in the loved kiss. The tongue, which now speaks but to chide, once knew no language but that of love. It was many Saturday nights ago, perhaps—but it was once. Why go to-night? Is there not some little corner in the heart where the old love—the old hope—the old pleasure lingers? Must you go to-night? Once you would not have left for an hour. Who has poisoned the feast? Who has bittered the spring? Talk it over this Saturday night. See who has shrouded the Pet and buried the Darling of years agone. Go not elsewhere for happiness. It is not to be found in the wine-cup. The glass of poison does not contain it. The allurements of the gaming-table give no happiness. Rest this night. If you still love, sit beside each other—eye to eye, at times—hand upon or in hand, at times. Read to her or him you love. Read this little chapter. It is kindly meant, even for those who differ from us. Look back and see how much happier you have been than you might have been—how much happier you might have been than you are. Do not blame. Do not chill the rivulet into an icicle.

Good wife, do not let him go. Make home happy for your own sake. Give him love for love—kiss for kiss—confidence for confidence. Be to him as you were when you won him. Call back the glance, the word, the old caress—the electric touch, and sit down together to bless GOD that you have each other to love and live for. Let new resolves be born to-night. They may die before another one comes around, but give them birth. GOD sent us here to be happy. We live to make ourselves miserable. GOD gave us Saturday night for love and reflection. He gave us the Sabbath for rest. He gave us six days for labor. And you, brother reader—comrade in life's battle, must you go from the home you have? It may not be quite pleasant, but can you not help make it so? Save your earnings. Save your heart. Save your manhood. Keep faith with yourself. Give this night to rest—to-morrow for worship, and give to GOD a heartfelt blessing for the mercies you have, for some Saturday Night will be your last!

CHAPTER XIX.

IN WHICH WE SPEAK OF THE ROADS, THE HEARTH AND FENDER.

AROUND the mountains—over hills —across plains more wearisome than toil in their monotony— through forests, deep, dark, and dismal — by pleasant homes and many-tongued groves—now smooth with turf-lined border—then rough and rugged with jagged rocks and rolling boulders, this roads winds its way. It ends somewhere, my boy—not up a tree; not on the brink of a yawning chasm; not in some grand, awful and majestic ocean, whose wondrous depths nothing but the OMNIPOTENT can fathom; not in little narrow, grave-like crevices. Yet it ends, my boy. Not abruptly and in a trackless blank, but, merging into some other road—the two becoming one—the identity of each is lost, and this, in turn, loses itself in still another—each one more beaten and travelled than the one we now are on. Valter, this road is typical of life. There are in man's brief existence cross-roads—hopes running into ours—our hopes and plans running into others—all forming a spider-like web of events, reaching far and wide. As the idle boy loosens one thread of the fine web of the morning spider, from some stake or bush—so does time and fate loosen a friend here—a friend there—but the falling threads catch on other points, and the beautiful web is upheld, repaired, and enlarged.

And, my boy, when life is over, it is not over. The track becomes a path—the path a byway; the byway a lane; the lane a road; the road a street. The road of life does not end in a grove

—it does not lose itself in the top of some bluff —in some dark chasm—but merges into and weds another life. More busy yet than this. We step from the path into the road—the path we so hated to leave—it is done in a moment, and we are amazed at the beauties bordering our new walk, and wonder that we wept to think others had reached its smoother track before us, or that we could dread to enter the road this little one leads into.

The road of life is one of trials, my boy. Few can walk without tripping or stumbling. Few are they who can walk and not weary—who seek not the shady side for the rest it gives. Why you and us walk, no one can tell. Why others travel, you and us do not know. The cars, boats, and stages are well filled—people have business in the city—aims as varied as the mackerel-back sky of autumn—each car, an archipelago of ideas, wonderful, inexplicable, and mysterious.

Man is like a trunk riding in a full baggage-car. The outside does not surely indicate the contents. The check is not always evidence of its destination—there are so many changes. Side by side we journey on, the humble satchel filled with valuable papers between two large trunks filled with stolen goods—the worn russet-covered valise cheek by jowl with the elegantly sacked storehouse of fashion. We see the trunks in the car—who claims them, you nor us, Valter, cannot tell.

And few of us know how to walk this road—or any other one. We go rattling along like a pauper cart—hub-hitting as do omnibuses in Broadway—striking posts and corners, jolting and smashing the delicate machinery of life, or wearing it out with too great friction. We travel too fast. We look so far ahead that we tumble. In the future the present is lost. Man never knows how he lives. Ambition is a cruel reinsman—up hill and down it drives the tired servant with stinging lash. Wealth is never won. The child is never satisfied with two apples in its tiny hand, but in grasping three, loses all. Revenge is sweet, but no one can ride with it long. Love is the most unreasonable motive, because it stops for neither ditch nor hedge.

Home is a good master, for the pay is good—interest prompt. Before we die let us look in upon one, my boy, and see if it is well to hasten on too fast. The hearth and fender look beautiful to the gentle. Ambition, even when gratified, cannot soothe pain or still the throbbing temple. Wealth never satisfies the heart. Fame is like the crumbling frosting to bridal cake—hard to make—easily broken. If there was a skylight in our final house, so that we could see who laughed and who wept when the sexton spat on his hands, grasped the shovel, and rattled in on our sonorous roof the first sod or mass of frozen dirt and stones—or if there were windows, so we could see who followed after with sad hearts, there would be satisfaction in death—but no. Words are cheap—they conceal one's thoughts.

The Roads, the Hearth and Fender. 143

Men call us friends—for fun. They use us as hunters do rifles—when gone, get another.

We pick up much rubbish as we look along through life, my boy—we learn much not worth learning—we cut the leaves to many a book of no benefit—we carry many a pile of slag thinking it to be virgin ore. We coil for use many a rope of sand.

But there is a light to life for all. There is a cushioned seat if we but use it.

By the Hearth and Fender.

When the toil is over, there you can enter. Some one heart from all of God's has run into your own, and side by side you sit and dream of the golden future. How like heaven are the Home bowers lining our path into the road beyond. The world may have all the day been cheerless—the cares of business may have been like the dew—the keen word, ungrateful act, or marked neglect may have cut to the heart—there is still one place left—Home.

Valter, my boy, it is a pleasant picture. The clanking gate opens the eyelids of some one within—the footstep on the walk falls on the ear like pleasant memories—the hand-touched door-knob stills for a moment the heart in waiting; the well-known presence *felt* by love lightens the load of the day—the word—the kiss—the gentle clasp—the lovelit glance revealing to each other treasures the world knows not of—the gentle drawing to your breast of the heart which so loves you—the sigh of relief as the heaven is reached—the kiss of love; more eloquent than words, more fervent than heat. These indicate a chapter in Life's great Book, but few ever read it.

Home is the place, my boy. Not the semblance—but the reality as God intended it.

When the labor of a long day is over, how blessed it is to have a HEARTH AND FENDER! The blast may howl without—casements may rattle—wagons may rumble—bells may jingle—dogs may bay at the cold moon—those you hate may plot for your ruin—the tempest may rage in fury; who cares? The labor of the day is over. Some one has kissed the last sorrow away. Some lips have thawed the frozen heart—some gentle hand has cleared from you the clouds of care which for hours have hung so dark and sombre over the heart. Some one, dearer than life to you, has nestled by your side, or sits in your lap with one arm around your neck; her soft cheek with electric touch setting your face in a tremor—eye looking home into mystic depths—happy! who cares for the world? Who cares for brambles lining the road?

The past pictures are one by one brought up—the future is bravely looked into—the present is improved. New life for the morrow is given. New hope for the future is yours. New wishes are born unto you. The hours of evening glide on. The heart all your own is gladdened by your loving presence. The minutes drop off like stitches from knitting-needles—lives run still closer in together, and you are happy.

And yet, Valter, with all these golden blessings to reward life, there are those who weary of existence and plunge over the deep precipice instead of following the road to its end; and there are those who see in the beautiful border of the daily road nothing but hate, envy, jealousy, and mistrust—who would die by the road, when it is so easy to reach the HEARTH AND FENDER.

CHAPTER XX.

Sunday Night.

TO-DAY is Saturday—to-night is Saturday night—to-morrow will be *Sunday*—after to-morrow is dead, and laid out in its black shroud, with the stars to guard and watch, Sunday night will come. Fix up the parlor —kindle the fire there early, so that the room will be warm—fill the lamp to the brim— see that the blinds or curtains are a *fit*—place the chairs at regular intervals about the room, like pickets—smooth the silken hair over the brow, and *wait*. A step! Ah! my little girl—

you know whose step! The heart trembles like a little bird—the eye wanders from object to object—and then to your own dear self. A rap on the door—a timid little rap! And you *pretend* not to hear it, though if it were made with a feather you would have heard it! Another rap—*ah!* by "hard" listening, you distinguish the sound. Singular! And how surprised you are, to be sure! Never dreamed of *his* coming! Take care, little one! Eyes talk louder than do lips! The parlor looks cheery. Two of the pickets are called in from the sides of the room. Of course your guest must be entertained. Time flies—the clock in the other room ticks away the moments—its hands slowly crawl up as if to peer over the door—the fire burns and crackles in its prison—the old folks file off to bed, to wonder what you are talking about, and to think of their sparking days—the clock talks its *take-care! take-care! take-care!*—now loud, then low—but your lips will meet and linger on the brink of love's fountain. The times are hard. The lamp wastes oil. What a pretext for economy! Its flame is turned down. Of course you cannot see as plain till the chairs come closer together. Hark! The faithful old clock, with its hands over its face so as not to see, says "*take-care*," but the hands will wander—the lips will meet—the eyes *will* go down into each other's mystic depths, lit by the purest of diamonds; and you wish that time did not fly *so* fast! The wood-box is empty! The solid glass has drank down the oil most wonderfully—the wick looks as if drenched in poverty—the murky morn peeps in through the crevices—you wonder where the hours have fled. Listen! The old clock says louder than ever, "*take-care*," "*take-care*," but again do you sip nectar from the ruby oval cup—your hands and eyes speak what the lips *have not time to*, and out on the old ocean of time floats Sunday night!

CHAPTER XXI.

IN WHICH WE TRAVEL ON DANGEROUS GROUND.

ALTER, my boy, take hold of my arm, and let us walk slowly, and speak very carefully, for fear that passers-by may hear.

"They will hear no good of themselves!"

Well, my boy, some of them would not, and some would. We will have to walk slowly, as the people are too slovenly to clear the snow from the walks in front of their houses, and it is dangerous to travel, except in the "horse-walk."

You are now, Valter, my boy, almost old

enough to marry. The nights are long, and it is pleasant to sit beside one you love, and to gaze into her soul-warming eyes--looking at the picture-gallery of the future. To love a girl, my boy, is a good thing, and God speed you in all such enterprises of the heart. But, my boy, look out. There is a "Jack for every Jill"—be sure you have the right heart, or better you had never known love. It is so easy to be miserable. Be careful, my boy, where your heart leads you to. You never can force a heart to love—love once lost *never* returns. Prayers, tears, entreaties, kindness, never will bring back the holy pleasure you once knew, if the current has changed.

If you are looking for a wife, Valter, my boy, you want a *woman*. You want to find one who will be a friend. One whose tears will mingle with your own—who will smile when you smile —who will love you, oh! so dearly. There are plenty of pretty flowers which give no odor. They will never pay for making into a bouquet.

There are humble little plants, growing low under hedges and beside little cottage-walls, which will yield a rich and lasting fragrance. These are the flowers to cull, and these repay the trouble of love culture. It is easy to let your heart run out—hard to reel it in. Be careful where it runs to.

If you go to see a girl, go with good intentions or stay away. And go to none but the good ones. Avoid coquettes—they are heartless and cold. There is a little girl in the house we have just passed. Monday night a fellow visits her. He sits on the sofa and talks nonsense till midnight—takes a kiss at the door and leaves. Tuesday night another chap calls—the parlor is again in use till the "wee sma' hour ayont the twal," and side by side they sit—his hand playing with the corner of her apron-string—his toe just touching the little slipper so prettily peeping out from her dress—his words those leading to love. At last he leaves, and his tobacco-stained lips have left their foul imprint on her cheek. Wednesday night another fellow calls. These are all nice young men of course—they visit the girl to make love to her. He sits beside her—his head half lying on her shoulders—his hand playing with the ring on her finger—at times playfully biting the stray curls which fall so gloriously over her pretty neck. Late in the night he leaves, and promises to call again. Thursday night another lover calls. The parlor is lighted up—the sofa is in use—her head rests on his shoulder—his arm is around her waist just as it is in these girl-ruining waltzes, where each libertine is allowed by polite society to hug every man's wife till the blood is frenzied. They talk low and forget what they say. He plays with the bows of her neck-tie—bites her finger nails in sport—tells her he is in love, and at past midnight the filthy fumes of gin can be tasted from her lips. Friday night another fellow goes to make love. He sits on the sofa—leaving room enough at the other end for a boy's coffin—he takes both her hands in his own—he holds her head close to his heart—he kisses over and over again the lips which should be sacred to some *one*—he clasps her about the waist and tells her he loves—he kisses her over and over again, and leaves for home to be saluted on his way by every chanticleer in the neighborhood.

Now, Valter, my boy, it is your turn Saturday night. That was the arrangement — go and teach your heart to love, enter the arena and bear off the prize.

"No, sir—I have got through!"

Right, Valter, my boy. Such a girl is not the girl to make a good wife of. It is time lost to win what you will wear with regret. The girl who really loves—whose heart is that of a true woman, wants no crowd of lovers. If she loves but one, she is wronging herself to tempt the others—if she loves all, she can love none truly. If you wish to be happy, Valter, my boy, keep clear of such decoys. She may love, but it is not of that kind which will last over the rough road to the grave; and in after years the prize you have won from so many competitors will not be as dear to you as when urged on by pride and ambition to win beauty and not goodness.

Let us tell you, my boy, who to win if you look for heaven on earth. Find some one whose tastes are like your own. The hearts of those who love will never be false—you will not have to woo to win. If you have found such a one, my boy, guard her with love—if not, wait till the throbbing heart and the eye answering eye, even the first time you meet, tells the story. Find one who loves you. Find one you can love, if all the world despise—find one your heart tells you is worthy, whom you will love—not because others do, but because she is the one you have always looked for—find the ideal of your dreams and childish fancies, and be happy.

Valter, my boy, there are such girls. These are those who will wait for one—who will live for one—who would die for one they love. They are not in the market for every one to inspect. They want no variety of love—they ask but for the heart that is true—the mind that is pure. When you have found such a girl, you have found a prize. Then, my boy, you will be happy. No matter if poverty is yours—love will share it. If sickness rests with you, love will lessen pain. Then, my boy, you can visit that girl, and talk over the future—can *wait* till the happy day that shall before the world make you her own protector, and give you a purpose to live for. You can go at night when the labors of the day are over, and how glad will be your coming! On the sofa—the lounge, or even on the uncarpeted floor, you can sit for hours, and, with no passion but holy love, talk over the future, and bless the day you first met. Distant may be the time when circumstances will enable you to take her to your own home—but it will come. Then, my boy, you can sit by her side, and the gently pressing hand—the softly beaming eye—the deep look which speaks volumes untold—the silent and pure kiss will nerve you on to a nobler life—to greater exertion—to purer aims. You will have no fear that others will drink of the nectar you in bashfulness did but sip—no fear that the secret wishes of your heart, known only to HER and GOD will ever be made known—no fear that another will break from the bush the rose you have so long watched and cared for.

Such a girl—one who wants but a single lover—but one to be the occupant of her inner heart, is worth a heaven. Win her, and love her. If you are poor and she will marry you, do it not, until able to support her, as sickness may rob your cupboard, but waiting can never break your love. If young, and she will wait, my boy, you have a prize greater than the Kohinoor. If in trouble and she still clings to you—weeps with you—sympathizes with you—kisses the tears from your eyes, and on bended knees you can together —heart pressing to heart—both hearts reaching up to GOD in prayer for His grace and blessings— look the future fearlessly in the face and swear to wait till the clouds lift; then, Valter, my boy, you have found an angel who will make your heart a paradise, and your life ever happy. Hearts are often matched, my boy—sometimes mated. And the car which carries all sorts of freight, is not a good car for pleasure parties.

CHAPTER XXII.

About Twigs and their Early Bending.

VALTER, my boy, it's a funny thing —about the twig, we mean.

"I don't twig it!"

Well, my boy—it is this: "Just as the twig is bent, the tree is inclined." No matter whether it be a wooden twig, or a meat one; a sprig of shillalah or a sprig of humanity. As you plant the corn, so will it grow, and it behooves people to plant straight. Now can you tell us, Valter, my boy, how a father—a fond and dear father, can expect his children to be amiable in their dispositions, when he is as cross as the gable end of a saw-horse whenever the house is graced with his presence? If the father swears, can he expect his son to refrain from the use of profanity? If he is cross and peevish, finding fault with everything and everybody, how can he reasonably expect the twiglets of his family to do differently? Leaning against the shrub will warp the tree, my boy. If the father keeps late hours, and frequents places like Cæsar's wife— beyond suspicion—how can he blame the son for following in the footsteps of his illustrious predecessor? If the father cannot control his temper, is it right, my boy, to whip the child for learning his daily lesson but too well? Little twigs see things very close. While the large tree is looking ahead over its neighbors; over stumps, rocks, creeks, valleys, and houses, the twig is looking close along the ground, twisting and bending about by every breeze, and prying into the little crooks, angles, and crevices, and under the leaves, stones, and bunches of flowers—ob-

"Whatever the parent does is right in the eyes of the child. Yet folks wonder why their children show certain traits of character as years settle upon them."—*Page* 161.

serving a thousand things its loftier parent never thinks of observing. If the father is a sloven, how can the child be anything else, until new ideas are born within him? If the father, on entering the house, throws his hat, coat, muffler, boots, and bundle in different directions, careless of the labor he makes for others, how can the child be chided for doing the same?

If the father is a church member, and, as is too often the case, succeeds in overreaching his neighbor, and boasts of it at the table—and the tea-table is a funny place, my boy—how can he expect his child to learn honesty, or to respect professors of religion? Whatever the parent does is right in the eyes of the child—yet, folks wonder why their children show certain traits of character, as years rapidly settle upon them. The mother expects her daughter to be a lady some day, but forgets to set an example. At the table, or by the fireside, she indulges in uncalled-for remarks about her neighbors, or throws out in sinuations against the character of those as good as herself, and then expects her child to be a lady! If the mother be untidy in her dress—allows dust and dirt to accumulate on stands and behind doors, how can she blame the daughter for falling into the same habit? If she washes the dishes in cold or lukewarm water, without soap, wipes them with a slowsy rag, and sets them away so greasy that you can draw Solomon's temple or write the epitaph of a baby in the grease on them with a fork tine, how in the name of faith can she expect her daughter to be neat? All these little things tell. These little twigs are great institutions, my boy, and the wind which sways the tree will affect the bush. Such is the law of nature, my boy. Yet folks never see it as they should. If the mother is a discreet and sensible woman, the daughters will be the same. If not, don't take chances on them, my boy. If the father is a gentleman, the son will be very apt to be much the same sort of a person, and take pride in honoring the author of his being.

There are a thousand little things, my boy, which will make the boy into a loafer or a man. There are a thousand little acts at home, the influence of which will never die. As the shadow reflects the image of the subject, either lesser or greater, so will children reflect the education of home; and the lessons taught by the fireside, or when kneeling by the side of a loved mother, last till we are no more. If a child is governed by kind words, so will its life give evidence. If home is made pleasant, the boy will have its sacred protection. If everything around the family circle is built loose and cross-grained, nothing but the power of God, or great ambition, will spring the boy back into the upright man. No one is fit to govern himself till he has been governed—no one can govern others till he can govern himself. And, my boy, it is the short lessons which we remember the longest. The home influences are seldom forgotten, and the lessons for good or evil which you and us received in years agone, when our minds were more susceptible than now, will make or damn us, my boy. Parents cannot be too careful of the little ones given them. Their home lessons cannot be too good.

If the parent thinks its own child perfect, how much more must the child think of its parent, and how perfect in its eyes must be all that parent does—how cherished the teachings, how indelible the picture the eyes of youth looked upon as correct! Yes, Valter, my boy, the twig is easily bent—but to straighten it is quite another and more difficult matter; and as some of our readers are so easy to take hints, we will leave the subject with them.

Now, Valter, my boy, you and us are both friends of the boys. They are to make our future men. Those boys we see in the streets late nights, running wild like pigs, will in time be a part of society. If they have early taught them habits of sobriety, of care, of self-denial, of respect to others, they will make good men, and honor the names of their parents. If they are allowed to run loose until their habits are set, no power except pride can save them. And by-and-by the fathers of these boys will see them either men taking an active, honorable, and influential part in life, or they will see them loafers, fit for nothing but to hold a chair down in some saloon. And, Valter, my boy, when death comes for his own, and the gray-haired man is laid down with *his* fathers, if his son who is to bear his name henceforth comes to his bedside, erect in the vigor of manhood, upright in character as in form, honest in heart, how easy will be the dying hours of that father, for he will know that the helpless ones left behind will not suffer. But if the son is called from some saloon, and comes in with unsteady gait, red, watery eyes, thick tongue, and maudlin voice, the picture will live with the aged man beyond the confines of the present, forever.

We like boys—the jovial, prompt-speaking, bright-eyed, willing, gentlemanly boy, who is early learning the true way to manhood. We love boys who mind their own business, who seek the society of good boys instead of bad ones, for such make our great and good men. We love the boy who is full of fun, but respects the feelings of others, for he is already a gentleman. But the boy who cares not how dirty his clothes, or soiled his face; who calls his father the "*old man,*" and the mother, on whose breast when an infant he found rest and peace, the "*old woman*" —who openly in the street tells his father he is a liar, and refuses to obey, is ticketed for a dishonored grave and dishonored memory. Parents, look to these matters!

To make men of boys, Valter, my boy, it is necessary they should be trained—not with a club, but by kind words, good examples, and little switches. If parents stay at home, keep good-natured, and make home pleasant, boys will love to gather round the fireside. Let them get papers and books and teach their children to read—let them have games in the parlor, and be welcomed with smiles. Make home attractive, and boys will stay there — make it a sort of quarrelling school, ornamented with unkind words, and boys will soon go to the devil by a more genial route.

CHAPTER XXIII.

In which a Hard Word is Used.

T seems very easy, but you and us know better. There are a million of people biding God's time, who have been ruined by not being able to speak it. There goes a hard-working man. A wife and three children are dependent upon his labor for bread. When he is sober he is as nice a man as there is in the world, but at times some careless chap who means well but is forgetful, asks him to stop labor and go on a spree. And then, Valter, that little word of two letters is so hard to pronounce, he cannot say it, and—the rest is too sad to tell.

And, Valter, my boy, here comes a man who once was rich. He had friends; and money; and a loving family; and position; and influence; and self-respect; and integrity; and a future of usefulness before him. But, my boy, he don't look like it now. He was elected to an important office. He forgot the lessons his good mother taught him, and was asked by designing politicians to sell his vote to a party of swindlers; he could not for the life of him give articulation to that little word, and so he fell.

And here, Valter, is a young man. Just like you and us, my boy. He has wit, sense, education, intelligence, friends, ambition, and is loved. He has a knowledge of the world, acquired by mixing with its people, and seeing with his own eyes its shades and sunbeams. He has ambition —and the same field in which to win honor, fame, and distinction as had Franklin, Fulton, Morse, and a host of others who have lived honorable lives and now occupy honored graves. He is naturally smart, but, Valter, my boy, as he meets us, do you see the excess of moisture in his eye—the little puffy ridge under it—the gradual turning of the beautiful corners of the mouth his mother so loved to kiss—the nervous, convulsive twitching of the hands? These, my boy, tell a sad tale—of early shipwreck—of disease—of premature death—of neglected and squandered gifts. He became what he is, because he could not think of that little word, till too late; and unless he thinks of it soon, it will be useless for him ever to try to do so.

And, Valter, my boy, here comes another man, whose nature is good—whose disposition is kind—whose wife loves him, but alas, Valter, he is not the man she married. Before the wedding, he was all attention—now he is so very clever, that no matter who asks him to go to some place of resort, even to the neglect of one whose smiles are worth more to his heart than is all else—whose happiness adds but to his own—he leaves his family circle till midnight or later, and the heart that once knew and loved him so well, is growing cold to him forever. He is a good fellow—clever—tells a capital story—makes a funny face, but, Valter, my boy, he can't say that little word, even for his own benefit.

And, my boy, how much better if teachers would educate children of tender and riper years to say "NO" at times. Not in a short, cold-iron—pipe-stem—bombshell style, but in a nimble, meaning way. If women, when sitting together and gossiping over the short comings or long goings of their neighbors not in earshot—would refrain from lying to and about each other—from trying to injure the characters of others as good as themselves—would in their hearts say, "No, I'll not do this thing," the world would be better off. And, Valter, when tempted to give the sharp word—the cross look—the sulky toss of the head—the unkind remark—the word that wounds—the glance that brings sorrow to those we love—how much better if we could mentally, if no other way, say "NO." Never say it, my boy, when prompted to do a good deed— when called upon to relieve the distressed— when asked to extend aid to those who are worthy—when prompted by your better nature to be kind; but when asked to take chances in the lottery of life which for reward only brings tears, sorrow, remorse, pain, guilt, and unhappiness, then with thoughts on the better angel who guards the door of your heart, no matter how great the effort, plainly and determinedly say "NO." It is a hard word, Valter, my boy, but it is one worth studying.

CHAPTER· XXIV.

MUSINGS AT THE END OF THE WEEK.

ANOTHER drop in Time's bucket! Another wave rolling in toward the shore of Eternity! Another chapter in the book of life! Another echo down the valley of Events! Saturday night! Look back over the leaves of the seven-volume book, closed never more to be opened this side the Great Unknown. Do you ever think, gentle reader, that each Saturday night closes the book for or against you? The week is God's Journal. The year is His Ledger. Death is His balance sheet, Debtor and Creditor! The week just laid in the "lap of ages" will unseal itself for your joy or your sorrow, as you alone have itemized the accounts. None of us have been perfect. Few of us dave done as we would that others would do by us. It is too late to recall the past, but not too late to pattern the future. Against some one, your hate has been strengthened. Your hate! Vain and deceptive word. How the grave mocks at your enmity against the soul it shelters. Of what use is it to hate each other? Surely life is not made pleasanter thereby. We are all but creatures. Mere leaves, borne to the earth by the breezes of time. Some fall sooner than others—but all of us fall. Leaf and thistle-down go by as merrily! They could not do otherwise. And what more is man?

Saturday night! How many a kiss has been given—how many a curse—how many a caress—how many a look of hate—how many a kind word—how many a promise has been broken—how many a heart has been wrecked—how many a soul lost—how many a loved one lowered to the narrow chamber—how many a babe has gone from earth to heaven—how many a little crib or cradle stands silent now which last Saturday night held rarest of all the treasures of the heart! A week is a life. A week is a history. A week marks events of sorrow or of gladness, which people never heed.

Go home to your family, man of business. Go home to your heart, erring wanderer. Go home to the cheer which awaits you, wronged waif on life's breakers. Go home to those you love, man of toil, and give one night to the joys and comforts fast flying by. Leave your books with complex figures — your dirty shop — your busy store. Rest with those you love; for God alone knows what next Saturday night will bring to you. Forget the world of care and the battles with life which have furrowed the week. Draw close about the family hearth. Gaze into the eyes of the heart-treasures God has given you. Be happy. Forgive those who have wronged you.

Shut from the heart, if but for one hour only, the corroding cares of life. The week to come will bring changes. The week just past has done so. How many a grave stands between this and last Saturday night! How many a heart is bitter to-night, which a week since was flushed and joyous? He is dead! She is dead! He is lost! She is lost! New loves have come—old ones are gone. Hearts once sad are now joyous. Hearts once joyous are now steeped in bitterness.

Saturday night! Go home to those you watch over. Leave the wine-cup—the poisoned glass—the carousing table—the room of revelry—the glances of tempters—the habitation of vice and profligacy, and for once, rest by your own friends, and gladden the hearts of those who, to your shame be it said, have for so many Saturday nights awaited your coming in sadness, in tears and silence. Go home to those you love; and as you bask in the loved presences, and meet to return the loved embraces of your heart's pets, strive to be a better man and to bless GOD for giving His weary children so dear a stepping-stone in the river to the Eternal, as SATURDAY NIGHT.

CHAPTER XXV.

IN WHICH POST-MORTEM PROCESSIONS ARE SPOKEN OF.

A STRING of carriages, Valter, my boy.

"Where?"

In your eye, Valter, too often. Boil it down—thrash it out—winnow it over—bag it up, deduct the commission, and the grand object of life is the *post-mortem* picture of a string of carriages. How it worries all of us! Whenever a good man, a bad man, or an indifferent man goes hence in a box, we look to the procession following him home—or to the threshold, and feel a touch of regret lest our procession will be a link or two shorter. This is a queer world, my boy. People care not for the living, while the dead are like incubated eggshells. The rifle-ball speeds on its way, and if death follows its flight, the marksman watching its passage laughs in glee. If a man makes his mark only in the grave, society smiles a sweet little smile, and is happy.

In Hindostan people are honest. The proof is in the fact that hired mourners follow men to the grave. Tears are worth their five tekels each. A bunch of hair, the size of a small trellett of asparagus, pulled fresh from the head of the professional brine-spiller, costs ten rupees. That is the country, my boy. That is the Edenic Garden of honesty, where funeralic elongations of the face are over with as soon as the initial clod bounces down with its hollow thump on the flat roof of the quiet tenant. This is a queer world, my boy. Men attend funerals as a matter of compliment. Not that the dead man will repay the little courtesy, but with the hope that such politeness will impress others with the style.

This is a quiet lane, Valter. Life is a lane, but not as quiet. While that funeral procession passed, you and us stood with uncovered heads. In France—wicked France, as they tell us—even the peasants pay this mark of respect to those who have only caught the notes of angelic choirs before them. Here, people do no such thin foolishness. It was a long procession, my boy. Longer than will wind along after you or us. Did you mark the look of those who followed? Noted you the manner in which the man with the bay horse toyed his whalebone among the weeds by the roadside, as if driving in from the races? And the two men in the next carriage—how they eyed the widow! The woman married for money, my boy. She got what she wanted. The poor fellow riding on his back, married for beauty. Oil and water. He died. She is free. Business, Valter—business is the word.

And the next carriage is a political debating school. The occupants speak low—the deceased had held an office—the grave will soon hold him—worms will open his heart into little worm-parlors—his veins will be canals—his once teeming brain will be a city of corruption—like all cities—the reptiles will feast on the office he left for greedy, sordid ghouls to feed and fatten upon. When a man is measured up, my boy, he doesn't amount to as much as a bale of rags. But his body—his brain, is the workshop from whence cometh beautiful machinery which will run for years after the shop is removed—or it is a mass of slag, boiled out by fire from the ore of humanity, tramwayed through life by the hand of fate. Side by side, lovers whispering joy — eye telling eye volumes too condensed for words. They are not mourning. The children of him who has hoed his row and left the weeds for his widow, mourn—to think the property to be divided is not larger. Political enemies ride in the procession, glad to think one object hateful to them is removed. Everybody goes to a funeral—except those who truly mourn. Mourning machinery would pay.

Valter, we have seen at home—after the procession had turned the corner, more anguish than all the mourners felt—we have known hearts that could not, for fear of what the world would say, go down into the waters of bitterness never to rise again. Secret and mysterious. Hid behind hedges—springing forth unseen by all save GOD, on the banks of the quiet stream, have bloomed flowers the world never knew of —but they bloomed, and died—*and lived again.* Deep in the aisles of nature—nestling under the mighty pines—trembling at the roar of the grand old forest—unseen and uncared for by the world, flowers have blossomed—have died when the storm was born and the tree which sheltered them so long, bowed in submission to His breath. Many a ball passes beyond the target and wounds deeper than time can heal—yet people but look at the mark. There is mourning, my boy, where we look for indifference—there is indifference where we look for tears.

Life is a curiosity shop—a pawnbroker's office—a medley of truth and falsehood. Men whistle on the streets—but they can never tell what tune! Others look at their watches, but in a minute after, in answer to the inquiry of a friend, cannot tell the time of day. Men write foolish letters, which, like Banquo's ghost, trouble them ever after. Some make promises whose children are regrets. They make friends whose teeth are outside their lips—who bite oftener than they kiss. Men are queer folks, Valter.

You and us, my boy, have much to learn. Death but takes the ticket we have spent our lives in making change for; and the show we attend beyond the vestibule will be in the pit or gallery, as we choose now. We live for nothing but appearances—anxious only to make the line of carriages appear as long as possible, but seldom know how to do it. Death comes to you and us—we are by the grave-yard "gobbled up"—the air which surrounds us gently comes together—no one cares for us then, except a few; yet, Valter, we spend our lives trying to please the multitude who know not our hearts nor will honor our memory. What a bubble we live on, my boy!

CHAPTER XXVI.

Pictures.—Picture First.

THE clock over the bar points to half-past eleven—within thirty minutes of midnight. Being in a city, the clock points yet to an early hour, but out by the little forty-by-eighty feet farms—out from the places of idle resort, that clock would point to a very late hour. Since tea-time, at a table four men have been sitting. Four mugs of ale—four gin cocktails—four cigars—four rum-punches — four brandy-smashes — four cigars—four mint-juleps—four whiskey-skins—four brandy-straights have been brought to that table since the sun bade us "good-night!" Full glasses to the table—empty ones back! The room has grown smoky—thick and foul. The hard chairs have become tired! The lamp begins to blush at the coarse stories told, in which the holy name of woman has been so often and profanely mixed. The brains grow dull—a weary morning approaches!

"Cut!"

"Let me shuffle first!"

"Spades trump!"

"Pass!"

"Pass!"

"By!"

"I'll take it up—bar-tender, another cocktail—stiff!"

"Well, boys, another rub on you! It's only twelve—let's have another rip!"

"Well, cut the papes! Clubs trump!"

"Pass!"

"Assist!"

"Play her alone—let her scoot!"

"Well, you made it—another brandy with sugar!"

"Rub apiece again! Let's saw for the cigars!"

"Stuck again — just my luck. Bar-tender, what's the pop?"

"Five rubs on you—five fortys—two dollars. Ten shillings on you! Dollar and twenty on you—two dollars on you—all right—take a cigar, gents, and call again!"

PICTURE SECOND.

"Eight o'clock, and he is not here yet! How dreary this little room does seem, and I am so lonesome! Ten o'clock! How I wish he would come. It's *so* lonely here with the children asleep! Once, he loved to stay with me, but now, alas! Twelve o'clock, and I am so tired. I cannot sleep! My heart aches and grows sad —I'm growing old, perhaps—maybe my face is not as fair as once, but my heart is as warm, though it is often sad.

"One o'clock! What charms can he find in that foul-scented room—by that dirty table, cutting and dealing those greasy cards—filling himself with poison—tainting his breath—ruining his mind—undermining his constitution—planting seeds of disease—squandering his money—clouded with smoke—tired with excitement! Is this happiness—is this life—is this our mission? Is this the realization of childhood's dreams? Oh! I am so tired of life—so weary of waiting and watching, that were it not for my babes I would go unbidden into the holy presence of my GOD! Morn comes, but not he."

"Has papa come?"

"No, my little pet—pa has not come—lie still!"

"If hot tears could add beauty to my face, none would be so handsome as I! But why will he not come? My eyes grow dim, my heart is in my throat—ah! I hear his footfall—weak and unsteady!"

PICTURE THIRD.

"Do you go down town to-night, my pet?"

"No, darling. I have labored enough to-day. Why should I flee from home—from happiness, from thee? Life is full short to love—too short to squander. I love the photograph of my heart too well. No, darling—my heart is here—here let me keep it company."

It is a pleasant room, but not a large one. Night has gently closed the windows of day, and set the golden seals as watchers over us. By an open window they sit, his head reclining on her breast; their hands linked together; their lips often wedded to each other, their souls going out together in the dim twilight, far into GOD's own future of love, and their lives so sweetly and calmly blending into the one that brings a happy reuniting in the beautiful spirit-world. Softly and lowly they talk over the past, and of the future—thanking God that they are man and wife—happy—*happy*—HAPPY. How her arms encircle his neck—how his arm clasps her heart to his own! With what holy love, for it is GOD's love, do they rest palm in palm—read their hearts by magic touch — study in beaming eyes the book of love—and from lips warm and red with life, slowly and gently take renewal seals of love and happiness! Many yesterdays have placed themselves as sentries between them and their wedding-day, but love has made no abatement. The day sentries have stepped one by one in, crowding that day back, and them on toward eternity, but love has been with them ever. No need of saloons to make the hours pass pleasantly, for where the heart is *anchored* there will be the world whose sun never sets, and at home will be found all the charms man can ask for. The heart *never* tires of one it loves. Each moment is as the one just past, only more precious. Heaven is within a man's own house if his idol be there, and his heart be true to its vows and manhood.

CHAPTER XXVII.

We Wonder why Wonders will never Cease!

ALTER, my boy, it is cold this morning. The snow, in fine particles, is sifting down on the just as well as the unjust. Draw your muffler close around your mouth—for a close mouth is a sign of a wise head.

"And a laughing man indicates an honest one!"

Well, Valter, my boy, that is the theory. But hasten on. It is yet early. All around you can see the white smoke going heavenward. It goes up, my boy, just as pretty—it curls as gracefully

—it floats off into the boundless air—it ascends as high toward the throne of GOD from the humble cabin of the laboring man, as from the tall chimney of the banker. Those columns of smoke are the morning freight-trains, carrying from earth to heaven the good and the evil thoughts of those who now, as we proceed to work, are gathering around their family hearths. And do you know, Valter, that at times it seems as if we could tell from the smoke of the chimneys, whether the ones who warm by the fire from which it rises are happy or miserable?

"How?"

Well, Valter, my boy, you notice, as we walk along, that from the little cabins of the Irish and German laborers—from the neat cottage of the honest working-man, the smoke rises more steadily—more clearly—more regularly than from other dwellings. So with their lives—their hopes—their wishes—their daily walk and conversation. Now look over there. That high, tucked-up chimney sends forth a whiffling, curly, unsteady, puffy-like column, resembling a corkscrew. It darts hither and yon. Can you see no resemblance there to the lives of those sleeping beneath its shadow, while a servant is cooking the morning repast?

"The higher it is the more it flirts and whiffles!"

That's it, Valter. On the tree of life, the higher you sit, the more unsteady are the branches! The bird in the topmost bough of the elm under which we are passing, when the wind blows, sits not half so steady as the one farther down. So with the tree of life. The higher one goes, the more he is tempted—the more the world buffets and storms about him; and unless his hold be firm—unless his heart know what integrity means, sooner or later he will fall. And, Valter, my boy, the higher you climb, the more care you should take to hold on! But, Valter, let us go in from the snow and storm. It is too much like the hearts of many we call our friends.

Ah! this is nice! So warm and pleasant Let us sit by the window and see others walk. Do you see that man, and that other man?

"Yes, but what of them?"

They are like other men, 'tis true, but they are not perfect. One is a father. He has three girls, all grown to womanhood. They are good girls —each one of them fit to make any honest, honorable man happy for life. The other man has a wife—a lady she is, too. They claim to be gentlemen—dress like gentlemen, bow to us like gentlemen, and gracefully salute us with the curving arm, as do gentlemen. But, Valter, my boy, if you should hear them in saloons—in bar-rooms, in little knots, in stores—everywhere; relating for the amusement of a dirty-minded crowd, stories, anecdotes, experiences, and lies, in which the holy and loved name of woman was so indecently mixed that you would term them, not gentlemen, but loafers.

How it sounds for *gentlemen* to get together and relate indecent stories by the hour! They are suitable persons to talk about women's "talking societies"! How they must respect women — how they must love the pure and innocent, to laugh until they cry, for hours together, over the coarse jest and low remark! Valter, my boy, GOD made man the strongest, to protect woman. Not alone by his strength, but by his silence. Not alone by force of arms, but the respect he should teach others to have for the sex who make life desirable. We look on our mothers, or on their memory, as sacred. We look on our wives, also, as sacred—on our daughters as pure and innocent. The true gentleman never speaks of woman, Valter, as other than she should be spoken of; and those who gather in cozy places to make her the subject of low remark and vulgar wit, make themselves less happy than they would be, did they not by their words and thoughts rob virtue of its sacredness—and by their conversation tend to make woman but a living piece of flesh, instead of the kind and precious creature of love—of goodness—of kind wishes and happy influences. And now, Valter, remember, that the true gentleman never speaks lightly of the one who gave him being, nor of her sex.

CHAPTER XXVIII.

Wherein the Use of Money is Spoken of.

"WALTER, my boy, you cannot eat it; it is not drinkable; clothing cannot be made of it, yet you and us toil and worry year after year.

"What for?"

"What for?" Money, to be sure. All there is in the world would be a goodly fortune, but my boy, it is not worth its cost. That is, for itself. Once in a while, my boy, a man gets enough, as he does of love, or any other passion, but the majority labor and save, and starve, and study deprivations, and go through life as an argument penetrates a fanatic, to get something to jingle while the devil is checking his baggage.

Money is a good thing; but then, my boy, not one in a hundred knows how to use it. There is happiness in it, if we know how to find it. Burying it in farms for poor men to dig out for us is not a good way. Hoarding twenty-five-cent pieces in a dirty stocking is no way to enlarge the heart. Carrying it folded in a belt around you is no sensible way. In God's heaven are many stars, but not more than there are ways to use money well and wisely.

Be liberal. Be a man—not a skinflint. If you have a talent, my boy, let it benefit some one. Give others the benefit of your light. Do not, because you are rich, allow your heart to become coated over with base metal. It takes but a little to support life—it takes but a little more to live well—and but a little more to live in good style. All beyond this had better be put to some good purpose. Don't be covetous, Valter, my boy. What if some old hunks are rich! Hot metal is, to our mind, a severe bed. Dispense the favors of life as you go. Help others and be happy.

What sense is there in carrying a big trunk to the depot—and there allowing it to remain? What evidence of wisdom is it to carry wealth to the grave—and then leave it? Where the streets are paved with gold, what little a man would get in this world, would be swept into the garbage pile. To be sure, you may die rich. That is, the editor who for a dollar and fifty cents writes your obituary in common style—for five dollars makes you a philosopher, and for ten makes you a Crœsus, will say you died rich, if a fortune was left for relatives to fight over. The ties of consanguinity, Valter, my boy, are regulated by the size of the oak chest. If the father is rich, you and us call him the old gentleman. If he is poor, we say "the old man." There is just as much difference in things as in persons, and some people know it.

We are rich, my boy, in our hearts—not in our breeches pockets. Coffins have no money-drawers, and if they had, it is too dark to make change *down there*. We shall be rich in the next world, or we shall be poor. And that is the world we are striving for. The papers say a man died rich. The Book above does not say so. There is nothing to his credit there, and he will have many debts to pay in the hereafter. The papers say he died poor. That means, here below, that when the administrator held his convention, there were causes but no effects. He died poor, and there were no lawsuits to hallow his memory. And the world pitied him. And the cows eat the grass and weeds from his grave, for he was poor. And the little hillock over which the lonesome sexton wiped the perspiration from a tired brow, like a dissolving view, became a little hollow. Yes,

Valter, my boy, he died poor. That is,—he was not in debt!

But in the other world, he is in good credit. He did not care to deposit in a land where the banks break twice a year, or pay in depreciated currency. And so he sent his fortune ahead— not all at once, as sailors fire a broadside, but a little at a time. He laid up treasure in heaven. Some of it was sent by a poor widow-woman, whose shanty down the road was no better than advice, to comfort her. A poor boy, without means to start in life and become a man before death, took to heaven an instalment for the man who died poor. And the sun reflected some of it right into the windows of heaven from the roof of an orphan asylum. And that poor old man, neglected and deserted by all save strangers, took a little HOME with him. And the little which saved a friend from ruin, went there. Little by little—day after day, it accumulated. On the rising prayer of the lone widow—by the grateful thought of the starving orphan—by the ideas of the scholar, little by little, none the less sure, every dollar others thought was wasted on earth, went to heaven and brought to him a greater interest than ten per cent. a month in advance.

You and us never know who die poor. None can tell the human heart, or where its treasures are. Riches are good, if we use them rightly. An idea will do to circulate—so will money. The circle is growing smaller and smaller, my boy. In a few days, we can stand in the centre and touch its farthest side. Then, Valter, the heart which is crusted over with gold pieces, as shingles are put on a house, will go down into the horrible darkness feeling so sad, and so lonely, that even "He died rich" will seem like a bitter mockery to us. Do good, my boy. That is the secret of life. Everything gives freely of its treasure but man, and everything else is happy. Cut the chain of care in twain, and let the sun of generosity find your heart. Don't take your money along, but send it ahead—and remember, Valter, my boy, you will keep it company some day. So be careful where you send it.

CHAPTER XXIX.

For Married Men, and their Wives.

"WHY do so many persons frequent saloons and other places of resort nights?"

Well, my boy, there are several reasons. Many frequent such places, but scarcely two from the same motive. The young men go there because they want fun. Married ones go to drown trouble. The old ones go because they have grown into the habit and cannot remain away.

There are times, my boy, when the heart is very sad—when every leaf of its inner book is bitterness. There are men who have wives—who have dwelling-houses—yet who have no *homes*. Men are not divine. Humanity is the substance from which sorrow's picture is taken. Weary with the labor of the day—tired of the perpetual round of toil and never-ending drudgery, many a time the heart of a brave man goes down under the waves of trouble, and there is hardly a glimmer of light in his horizon of days or years. He goes home to meet his wife. He opens the gate and steps within the little enclosure which should contain his heart's **treasure** and the joy of his life. He ascends the steps. He turns the knob or lifts the latch. He is in the once hoped-for wish of his life. There is no smile of welcome for him, but plenty for others. The marital fortune is made! The world is cold, my boy. It is a grave moulded in ice—more inhospitable than though it were in an arctic iceberg.

Men hunger for love. Men yearn for the kindness and affection which in dreams they have seen, and when they go to the well and no water is there, the heart becomes as lead and the spirit like the black wings of death.

But few of us, Valter, are really happy. There is a source of power in every piece of mechanism. There is a cause for joy or for grief in every heart. The world may not know it—it is no business of the world's what it is, but it is there. Men see the smiles their hearts crave, budding only for them, but full blossoming for others, and hell itself is paradise compared with the poignancy of sorrow which takes the soul captive. The prize they hoped for is not always there. The kind words they have waited till night for—have walked in weariness for—is not there when wanted. The sun which was in thought to have driven the sombre gloom from the soul had no light or warmth for the one who needed it more than all the world beside.

The world never sympathizes—never feels for

sorrow, but, like the prickly vine, sends its points into every heart to wound and torture, then gloat over the pain it has caused.

It is the lack of home sympathy that drives men to places they would not otherwise frequent, my boy. It is the lack of the relying love they hunger for which makes the world endurable. It is the fact that when all looks dark to them, there is no *home*—no constancy of love—no firm anchor to the heart on which their ship can drag for an hour till the storm is kissed or soothed away.

We cannot, every one, be all in all to each other. There is but one GOD for us, my boy. There is never but one heart which seems like heaven. There are never but one pair of arms which can shield the sensitive heart from sorrow —there is never but one voice whose low melodies can enchant the spirit and rescue the weary soul from the gloomy captor in whose keeping it is for the time. And, my boy, when that hope fails—when the last harbor the storm-tossed voyager makes for is closed against him, or so crowded with others that there is no room for him, the darkness of midnight is noon—the howlings of the hurricane are zephyrs—the angry flashes of God's lightning but love-glances—the goadings of sorrowing despair the white arms of love by comparison.

We blame people too much. But few of us pity. Too many censure where they should keep silent if they cannot sympathize. It is not for us to censure—God does that. It is for us, my boy, to love and be true in heart. It is for us to dispel all the gloom we can. In the spring-time how carefully is the ground prepared for the seed or plant; and be it fruit or flower, every moment's care and attention given it repays the kind hand and loving eye with its choicest riches in proportion to the love, care, and labor bestowed on it.

We cannot love too much if we love well.

Heaven is love, and surely we cannot take too earnest lessons in the principles thereof. And, my boy, when you see a man away from his home—seeking elsewhere, not for pleasure, but for that in which sorrow can be drowned, deal not with him in thought too harshly. GOD knows he suffers enough, else the friends would be his earthly paradise and the vexations of the day which by night are harvested in a pile of trouble in his heart would be chased away by the love he needs to strengthen him for the morrow's toil. Men will not be long absent from those they love. It is not in nature. If they are absent from choice, how desolate must be their hearts—how tear-calling their thoughts!

Men care too little for their wives. Wives care too little for their husbands. The heart that was once won is not kept. The pleasures of the chase have drowned out the enjoyment of the possession—the market once made, the window is emptied of its attractions.

And so we live on, my boy. The hills of happiness vanish into thin air—driven away by our own acts, and the plain over which we daily walk becomes a desert of arid thought—a road filled with dead-falls, for the reason that we are too busy performing for dead-heads in preference to paying patrons. There are a few in life who have learned the secret in the last sentence, and they are happy. Outside attractions dazzle not their eyes or lure their hearts—outside threats have no terrors, and loved and loving they go on to eternity in happiness.

CHAPTER XXX.

IN WHICH BOYS AND APPRENTICES ARE SPOKEN OF AND TO.

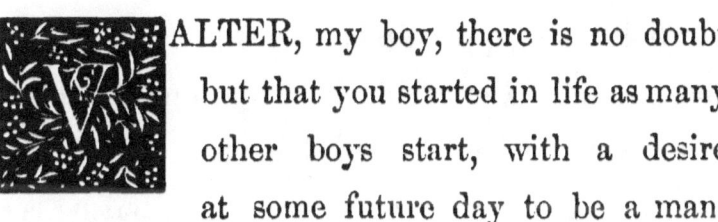ALTER, my boy, there is no doubt but that you started in life as many other boys start, with a desire at some future day to be a man. That, my boy, is a good target to shoot at, but somehow or other lots of boys miss by shooting too quick. Much good powder is wasted by such foolishness—much game is flushed and flown by over-eagerness. You have just started out on the road of life. It is a hard one to travel. You and us, my boy, have both passed by several

annual mile-stones—we have passed by the most —have seen the most joy and sadness—the most success and failure as yet, my boy.

You are learning a trade. That is a good thing to have—it is better than gold—brings a larger premium. But to bring a premium, the trade must be perfect—no plated-silver affair. When you go to learn a trade, do so with a determination to win. Make up your mind what you will be, and be it. Do not whiffle around, but hold your upper lip close down, and labor for the future. Determine in your mind to be a good workman, or let the job out. A botch is not only a disgrace to his profession, but he is a disgrace to himself and a mighty poor advertisement for his father.

>Bide your time,
>Learn to wait.
>Learn to labor—
>Trust in fate.

Ever honest—
Keep your pluck.
Ever faithful—
Trust in luck.

It is easy to succeed if you but will it. Have pluck and patience. Look out for the interests of your employer—thus you will learn to look out for your own. Keep an eye out, and do not wait to be told everything. Remember. That is a big word, my boy, in the dictionary of success. Act as though you wished to learn, and some one—no matter who, will show you how. Learning a trade is different from eating mush and milk. Mechanical education does not slip down without chewing. If you have an errand to do, do not move as if you were training a sloth, but start off like a boy with some life. Acquire the habit of activity, if you have it not. Look about you. See how the best workman in the shop does—copy from him.

And, Valter, my boy, learn to do things well.

Whatever is worth doing at all, is worth doing well. Never slight your work—never. Every job you do is a sign. Poor signs are useless for good. If you have done a job in ten minutes, try and see if you cannot do the next one in nine. But, my boy, never be in too great haste. Too many boys spoil a lifetime, by not having patience. They work at a trade until they see about one half of its mysteries, then strike for higher wages.

We hate a Rat.

A rat, my boy, is the mechanic who has half learned his trade, and then works at half regular wages. Such folks are poor eggs. We see them every day—men who are to their professions what a wart is on the hand—a three-legged chair at a prayer-meeting—a lame horse in an elopement. If you undertake to learn, do it. Learn well, or not at all. Be a workman or a corpse—do not, for your own sake, be a botch, only able to earn half wages, and never able to keep a situation longer than it takes a goose to hatch a family. A poor hand among good ones is worse off than the fifth calf. For the sake of a year's time, do not lose the entire future. When learning a trade, my boy, don't move like a rusty watch. Act as if your interest and the interest of your employer were the same. Employers will not willingly lose good employés. Be honest and faithful. There is the secret of success, my boy, and that is the great thing lacking with too many. And, Valter, my boy, never get above your business, nor take style too thick.

Never leave the table hungry if there is enough to eat. It spoils the day for labor. Never leave a girl half sparked. Some amateur will commence where you left off, and away goes your sweetness on the deserted heir. Never chop a stick of wood half into and then leave it—never draw a bucket of water half-way out of a well and then let it back—never half learn a trade. All such transactions are labor lost, and show very thin brains. If you play, play for "keeps," in such matters. If you are aiming to be a man, be one, or quit. If you are learning a trade or profession, learn the whole of it. When you commence being man, it is time you left off being boy, to a certain extent. It looks bad to pick the raisins out of pies and leave the rest, but that is not so indicative of a platter-head as to see one of these half-hatched mechanics or professors, not able to do a job of work without an instructor.

Good mechanics are the props of society. They are those who stuck to their trades until they learned them. Poor ones are living nuisances—and they are the rats who quit in boyhood from over-smartness. Go slow and sure, my boy—that is the only safe way. People always speak well of a boy who minds his own business—who is willing to work, and who seems disposed to be somebody in time. This is a queer world—many people are watching us, my boy, and help often comes when and from where we least expect it. Confidence is the safe in which men often deposit rich treasures, and as you and us, my boy, prove worthy, so will we be rewarded. And, Valter, since the day God looked upon the work of His six days and said He was well pleased, man has had the fullest liberty to exult over *his* success. God used those words for some purpose, and if He felt a pleasure in saying what He had done, how much it promises for all who build a monument, be it high or low, and from its summit themselves behold the crowd following along in the path they have carved out, or climbing the steps they have carefully erected! There is a rich reward in success, which none but those who strive can ever enjoy.

CHAPTER XXXI.

Wherein my Boy is counselled to Mind his own Business.

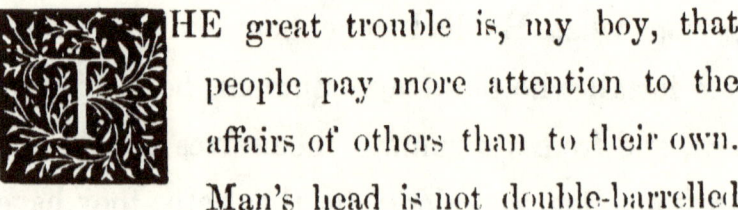HE great trouble is, my boy, that people pay more attention to the affairs of others than to their own. Man's head is not double-barrelled like a shot-gun. God gave every man a head of his own, and he who attends to his own business has enough to keep him busy forever. People are like wasps. Society is a sugar-barrel with the sweetness taken out. Meddlers go buzzing and bunting their heads against the soured sides. There are thousands who know nothing of their own business, but know all about the concerns of

their neighbors. We all despise such folks, yet fall into their errors. We say they are fools— and they are, my boy—and yet adopt their peculiarities. Each man has a duty—it is to himself, and through himself he benefits others.

Tearing another's character to pieces will not help ours. Pointing out the weeds in your yard will not make the weeds in our yard more beautiful. Censuring others publicly for faults we are guilty of privately, will make us no better, nor ever elevate society to a higher plane than is now occupied by it.

There is no perfection on earth, Valter. The rainbow is but a part. The day is half night. The sun gives the shade. The deeper the water the more beautiful the reflection—but it is not the more perfect. There is no picture without a background. What we condemn in others are the faults to be found in our own hearts. Where others have failed in part, you and us might have

Minding one's own Business. 221

failed totally. Every street is full of filth. Every fence is full of nails. Tear the boards or pickets off, and the rusty heads protrude to rend the beautiful garments which in turn cover mental deformity. The white cottage and the brown mansion hide trouble from the world. If walls could speak, thousands who now listen would stop their ears in anguish. If the whole truth of each of our lives was known, few are there living who would not seek a strange land. If each act of life was engraven on the forehead, thick veils would be worn by men and women, and their dying requests would be to refrain from lifting or removing them.

People talk, my boy, and know not whereof they speak. They retail slanders and scandal, to show how foul is the dish most palatable to them. Let you and us, my boy, walk straight along. The path is narrow. Brambles border our road on either side. If we do not stop to rest on their points, little will they molest us.

Let us each mind our own business, and you nor us will ever be out of employ.　*　*

Did you notice the guide-board we just passed, Valter, my boy? For years has it stood there, truthfully pointing the way. No harm has it ever done. Some wanton fool, from a kicking old gun, sent a charge of shot, marring, peppering, and scarring its truthful face. As fools with loaded guns passed, unable to find game, each one let fly one or both barrels, to see if he could not add a few black marks to the honest board. There was no cause for this wantonness. Make the comparison, my boy. Many a man—many an honored woman—has stood for years, the target of slander, yet swerved not from the strict line of right and honor. It seems, my boy, as if every prominent object, animate or inanimate, must be the mark for fools to fire at.

There is a secret in everything. We cannot tell why the wind blows, why the snow falls, why God exists, why eternity is endless, why

"As fools with loaded guns passed, unable to find game, each one let fly one or both barrels, to see if he could not add a few black marks to the honest board." —*Page* 222.

frost locks and heat unlocks the bountiful storehouse of Nature ; why man came on earth, why he leaves it ; why birds are hatched and babies are born, why flowers bloom and trees decay, why water flows and earth is firm, why night is dark and day is light, why vice follows civilization as a child followeth its mother, why death follows disease, why strife follows anger or love follows friendship, why disgust often follows indifference and revenge follows insult, why old age follows manhood, success exertion, want prodigality, or hope follows fear; why man does this or fails to do that. It is enough for us, my boy, to know that these things are so. There is a secret reason for every action, a secret chamber in every heart ; and we should thank God that we have even the ability to mind our own business, whether others do or not.

And remember, as we walk along through life, that random shots are never counted, and that the targets oftenest fired at are the most prominent ones. Remember this, and that he who minds his own business builds a wall about himself which no shafts can penetrate; and remembering this, one secret of success and happiness is yours, my boy.

CHAPTER XXXII.

In which we Speak of Something that Concerns Somebody.

ALTER, my boy, never drive a setting hen from her nest. Never pull up a plant that is growing, in order to see why it does not grow faster. Let well enough alone. Some flowers bloom earlier than others—but, my boy, it is not the early fruit that lasts the longest. A quick word is less terrible than nurtured anger. The snow that melts as it falls is not the snow which freezes the child and man. A man seldom knows when he is well off. The disposition of the heart is to err—to wander—to worry over lesser evils.

till at last it is wedded to the very troubles it hoped to avoid. If you have a good thing, stick to it. Do not let go of a cord to grasp a cable. So long as the cord holds, it is all you want. If you are near the earth, and the cord breaks, you will not be greatly injured by the fall. If far above, the risk of catching the cable is equal to that of the breaking of the cord.

If your home is happy, stick to it. If your heart be right now, keep it so. If you have one true friend, cling to him or her. Many a man and woman have hosts of false friends. If you have a plan that promises success, work it out. If you know one heart that is true to you, do not lose the love therein by act or word—by sin of omission or commission. Do not move away from trouble merely because it exists. If you cannot conquer it on your own grounds, you cannot elsewhere. To fly is to fear; to fear is to court defeat; to court defeat is to be unworthy a good name.

In love or business it is the same. The sunglass burns into the hardest wood in time—only hold it steadily. You may see in a friend that which is not quite right. Would your next friend be more perfect? You may have failures in business—would a new battle with strangers be better for you? You may lose a few friends—are not the ones who are tried and true of more account than all the world? If your bed rests you, it is a good one, even though coarse and plain. It may not suit others—but if it suits you, keep it. Do not throw away a dime because it is not a dollar. The dollar, when gained, may be bogus; and if the dime supplies your wants, what more? Prove that which you love. If it has served you well, do not part with it. If not, let it go without a murmur. There is a mate for everything but despair. The flowers peep out from behind rocks—they lift their dewy faces to the light, and nod to each other. The tiniest one that blooms is as fragrant as the largest, in pro portion, and often more fragrant. The drop falling in the river weds its mate, and passes on. The breeze from the bower, bearing away the zephyr, is content with its choice. The ivy, clinging to the oak, is satisfied—for the oak will surely uphold in every storm. The willow bends low to toy with the bird—each to the other a friend. The grass stoops to kiss the stream—it kisses it again and again—it pillows itself on the icy shroud in winter—it retires from the world in January, and drinks from its hidden life in happiness—it throws its points of love far over and into the rippling wavelet in summer again, and each lives in the other constantly. The stream gives life to the blade—the blade shields its pet ripple from the glare of the sun, as the love of a true woman shields and protects the heart of him chosen beneath the trysting-tree, from all his fellows. Remove the plant, and the laugh of the rill dies by evaporation—its voice will never be heard in the great roar of the sea—turn aside the stream, and the blade withers and sinks in sorrow to the earth.

Have you one friend? How many there are who have none! Is that one friend true? What more is necessary? Heaven has but one God. The year has but one summer. Life is not all vernal. The watch has but one mainspring. The voice has but one echo. Life hath but one death. The needle points to but one North. The heart will live in such happiness that the world may well envy it, if it basks in the spiritual sunshine of one counterpart. Wait. Have patience. The dimes will be dollars, if not by growth, by premium! The shadow which is at your feet now is moving steadily away from you. The great resting-place is drawing nigh. Do not risk a certainty for an uncertainty.

Look about you, my boy, and see if there be not many others in worse plight than yourself. Your home may not be a palace, but it is a home. What more do you want? Learn to love that which you have. Learn to bide your time. There is a day for every night. If there are six months of darkness, six months of light are sure to follow! Be a man. Deserve success. Be true to your heart and to your word—be true to your friends and to your purpose. This is the great secret of life. How few know it, my boy! What if the world laughs at you? Does the world have terrors for you? Are you not the equal of your fellow? GOD alone rewards. The teacher, not the scholars like yourself, is the one who punishes.

Learn to succeed in great things by succeeding in little ones. Learn to be happy in well-doing. Study to make a bower in but one place in the wilderness. Plant your roses and ivies in but one place—water them—care for them—watch them—think of them—protect them, and never will you lack for a dear resting-place. Wait. Go slow. Learn the road. Study life. See how few of God's children succeed, see how few are happy. See how few are contented. Contentment is the anchor of life. Ambition the spur. When the storm comes, seek shelter. When all is pleasant, beautify your home without. When the heart of her or him you love is sad, chase the gloom away—smother it in kisses or care. When the heart is glad, rejoice with it, and revel in the sunshine you have helped create! Haste is not speed. The glare of the sun is not as sweet as the evening zephyr. The queen is not happier than the cottager. The desert is not as attractive as the oasis. The ocean is grand, but a home by the rivulet is dearer, my boy.

CHAPTER XXXIII.

We Converse on how Men may Succeed.

VALTER, my boy, do you realize that each year the grave is nearer you than ever before—that unless you are active, the season of life will close before even half your self-allotted contract will have been performed, unless, like too many people, you have no aim—no hope—no ambition beyond picking your teeth after dinner? Half of the world—yes, Valter, more than half—go to the reception-room of eternity without any object in life—as drift-wood floats down the stream, guided by the current, and lodging against the first obstruction. And what is drift-wood, my boy? Once in a while a good stick of timber is found therein, but it is generally more work to haul it out, clean off the sand and mud, than it is worth; and more time and tools are spoiled in making it into what you wish than the stick will ever bring, even in an active market.

Have a purpose, my boy. Live for something. Make up your mind what you will be, and come up to the mark, or die in the attempt. This is a land where there is no stint to ambition. All have an equal chance. Blood tells—pluck wins —honor and integrity well directed will scale the highest rock, and bear a heavy load to its top. Do not start off in life without knowing where you are going. Load for the game you are hunting. It is as easy to be a man as a mouse. It is as easy to have friends as enemies—it is easier to have both than to go through life like a tar-bucket under a wagon, bumping over stumps, or swinging right and left, without a will of your own. Every one can be something. There is enough to do. There are forests to fell—rivers to explore—cities to build—railroads to construct—inventions yet to be studied out—ideas to advance—men to convert—countries to conquer—women to love—offices to be filled—wealth and position to acquire—a name to win—a heaven to reach. Yes, my boy, there is lots of work to do, and you and us must do our share.

The world is wide, and its owner is God. If you wish to be somebody, "pitch in." The brave always have friends. Where there is a will there is a way. Where others have gone you can go. And, Valter, my boy, if the old track don't suit—make a new one—somebody will walk it. Success is never obtained in a country like this, without effort. If you fail once, try it again. If you fall down, get up aga'n. If it is dark, strike a light. If you are in the shade, move around, for if there is a shade on one side, there is sunshine on the other!

If your seat is too hard to sit on, stand up. If a rock rises before you, roll it away, blast it, or climb over it. It takes longer to skin an elephant than a mouse—but the skin is worth something. Never be content with doing what another has done—excel him. If an enemy gets in your way, knock him down, or push him aside. Deserve success, and it will come. The boy is not born a man. The sun does not rise like a rocket, or go down like a bullet fired from a gun. Slowly but surely, it makes its rounds, and never tires. It is as easy to be a leader as a wheel-horse, and you are then always the first in town. If the job be long, the pay will be greater—if the task be hard, the more competent you must be to do it.

And then, my boy, always be honorable. Keep your word or give a good excuse. If you owe a man, pay him, if it takes all you have. If you cannot pay—you can say so at once. Do to others as you would be done by. Punish enemies and reward friends. If you do not punish enemies, no one will fear you—if you fail to reward friends, we pity the selfishness of your heart. If you make a promise, keep it. If others betray you, teach them better; but on no provocation become a betrayer. If you have a secret, keep it closely—if it is the secret of another, watch it even more closely than your own. There can be no excuse for a betrayal of confidence—no apology that can be sufficient. If you are in hard luck, wear it out. If you can help a friend, always do it, if he is worthy—if you cannot, do not insult him in the manner of refusal. A little word, act, or look, when the heart is sore, lingers as does the fragrance of the rose long after the vase is broken. If you are right, maintain it. If wrong, never be ashamed to own it. Keep your head above water, no matter how deep the stream or swift the current—somebody will help you. Do not grumble, fret, or whine. Dogs whine. It is as easy to be cheerful as to snarl, and a good-natured man always makes the handsomest corpse.

Do not change your business every time you have the blues—change is not always beneficial. If you have been cheated, do not, to get even, cheat some one else. If you have made a bad bargain—do not stop trading, but try to make a better one next time. If you get into a scrape, extricate yourself, and look closer next time—never be caught twice in the same trap. People may forgive errors, but they have no sympathy for fools. If you wish to be a leader—*always go ahead*—and remember that the smoother the route you select, the less complaining there will be among your followers; and above all, Valter, my boy, no matter what the circumstances, never be the first to desert your friends. Be honest and faithful—GOD and good fortune will never desert you long.

CHAPTER XXXIV

WE TALK OF THINGS WE OUGHT NOT TO TALK OF.

WALTER, my boy, it is late to-night. We have been out in the cold a long distance, and have passed many dwellings. And, my boy, do you remember the neat white house, just by where we met the fancy dog with his pretty blanket?

"What, the house where the folks were quarrelling?"

Take care, my boy, that is not it! You speak too plainly! That was not quarrelling—only the good wife scolding. That is her way. She cannot help being sharp with her tongue, no more than a lame horse can help limping. A few years since, when she was led to the altar, a blushing bride, she never thought of such a thing. She was a sweetheart then. She wanted a husband. She got one—a good man, but like all people, with some faults. And do you know, Valter, my boy, that God never made but one perfect! She loved her husband, but the trouble was, when one was vexed—the other became more so, and the kisses soon changed to tart words, and the heart became crusted over with a sort of *dead* feeling, as the pail of water, when the night is cold, grows a coat of ice.

"That is what makes folks miserable?"

Yes, Valter, my boy, the *dead* feeling is what does it? The husband married his wife because he loved her. He married that woman when a girl, because he wanted a heart to confide in—a bosom on which to rest his aching head when weary with business—her soft hand to pet him— her warm kisses to re-nerve him with new life--

her smiles to welcome him home—her look of love when the heart was too happy to speak—her prayer for him when tempted—her loved person to care for, guard, and protect with the holy love a true man feels. But, Valter, my boy, the cold word startled him. It was an ice-water bath when warm with love, and his heart took in one of its feelers. Then, when the next cross word came, it was colder. His heart shrank back still further. The dream of youth was not realized. The treasure his heart had carried so long and far to the bridal, melted little by little, as ice melts in the summer sun, and his hopes ran out in such little streams that they were all lost!

Now, my boy, he lives there in that white house. She gives him more scoldings than kisses, and he is *waiting*. Home is not pleasant to either. He comes to its sacred portals late at night, because other places are more inviting. While away, he escapes the words which make his heart sad, and over the maddening bowl loses sorrow in oblivious torpor. Neither are happy—neither have the courage to start anew—or to love each other and be happy again. He married an angel—she was but a woman! She married a man—he was but human!

"This world don't amount to much."

That is so, in one sense, my boy—you and I are but atoms—less than grains of sand. But few, if any, really love us—we live a few years—die—are buried to be got rid of—and the world goes on as before. Those we loved forget us—our hopes die with us—the labor of a life is lost—the dream of youth is gradually stripped of its beautiful visions—and we are dead. We may live in white houses and not be happy. The one we love, by unkind words may chill the heart only too fondly her own. Woman was made to love. That is her mission—her wealth—her heaven. Man was made to protect—to love—to cherish. His hand is hard and against every man's. His heart grows cold and metallic as it is knocked about from day to day—his head becomes wrinkled as trouble lights upon it. Yet he labors on and is happy. All he wants is to fully realize that he is working for some one. If he is a selfish man, he works for himself alone. If he is really noble, he labors for one who repays his labor by her love, and is happy. But, my boy, when the one he worships allows her lips to furnish tarts instead of kisses, his heart loses courage. Woman never speaks harshly to the one she loves, and man knows it. The man never forgets himself and speaks in angry tones to the chosen one from all the world, until love has raised anchor and is ready to fly.

CHAPTER XXXV.

We find Where to Look for Happiness.

ALTER, my boy, the old chap who made adages said, that a contented mind was a continual feast. He was a very good adage-maker, but his advice was much as would be that of a man who might give you a safe full of money, and not tell you how to unlock it. The chief end of man is happiness. But very few men are happy, my boy. That is, they are not happy to-day, but expect the full measure of bliss to-morrow. To-morrow is a great day, Valter. One to-morrow has more of fear or more of happiness than all

the to-days ever almanacked. We all look for happiness—not in the present, but in the future—and, my boy, we are all wrong. Happiness makes us enjoy life. We can all be happy if we will. Care is the huge grindstone which wears us away. The knife does not wear by use—it is by grinding. Throw care and fretting to the winds. Now is the time to be happy. What is the use of waiting till another day dawns?

"How can we help waiting?"

Easy enough, my boy. Keep the heart right. That is the first point. If you see a man in trouble, help him out, if you can. If not, do not push him into deeper water. If you are tempted to do a mean act, stop and think how it will belittle you. If you see trouble, alleviate it. If you see a man in danger, tell him of it. Plant good seed—reap good crops. Be kind to others. Follow the golden rule. Make up your mind to be happy—the rest is easy enough. We have but very little real trouble. Most of it is imaginary. We become nervous and fretful, and weeds of care overrun the garden of the heart, where they should never be allowed to take root.

Now is the time to be happy. Think of the blessings, not of the curses. Look on your successes, not on your failures. Thousands fail —any one can do that; but to succeed requires a man of pluck, muscle, and ambition. So long as we have health we should be happy. And if sick we might be worse off, my boy. If we have but a dollar—we might have none. If but one suit of clothes—we might be a hundred per cent. worse off. If an eye has been lost by accident, remember that the head might have gone, for all you could do to prevent. If in battle, and a cannon-ball just misses your head, think how lucky that you were short. If it goes through your heart, a lingering sickness and sorrowful death-bed scene have been escaped. If you have one friend left, that is better than to have none—if you have none, you will not be betrayed, or you can make friends. There is no man so mean but some one will love him. Be happy in thinking of what you have—not in what you want. Let envy go to the wind. Think how much better off you are than a score who started in life with you. Think how much better off than you might be. Don't let trifles worry you. Keep a stiff upper lip, and a close lower one. The lower lip is the one you should guard—it does the talking.

It is easy to be happy if you wish to be, my boy. Gold watches—fast horses—iron fences—monthly dividends—Brussels carpets—rosewood doors—marble-top bureaus—eight-story houses—silver napkin-rings — squeaking shoes — poodle dogs—wine suppers—palatial residences, and such gewgaws, although nice to have, are not essential to happiness. If you are single, my boy, you can be happy in seeking some one to love you. But do not be in too great haste to better your condition. Go slow. You will see more of the country—may like it better. A well-trained mind—a kind heart, will make every one happy. If you have not these things, cultivate them. Make a little heaven in your heart and see how nice it is. Do not care what others say of you. If they flatter, try and come up to their mark of adulation—if they condemn, give them no more reason—if they censure wrongfully, it is a blessed thing to know somebody besides yourself is in error. Look around, my boy, and see if there is not some little spot where you can plant a kind word. It will bring forth a rich crop. See if there is not some breeze passing which will waft a kiss to one you love. See if there is not a place vacant where you can hide a good action. See if you cannot by word, look, or deed, brighten the heart of some one more miserable than yourself. Do these and be happy. And all can do those little things. We are made in the image of God, and surely, when He has placed happiness here on earth, we ought to help ourselves. Never care to look at the dark side of a picture. If there is no bright side to it, look on another one. If there is no bright side to any of them, paint one, even if with a whitewash brush. Make up your mind to be happy at all events—to take trouble as it comes, and part with it as it goes, and you will be fat and hearty twenty-five years after your grouty neighbor has put on his wooden overcoat.

CHAPTER XXXVI.

Another Week Gone.

By the light of the stars lay it away in Time's grave. Another week—another Saturday night—another flake covering the past with its mantle of forgetfulness. Another balance-sheet for or against us. Another seed planted over our grave to bring forth a flower around which beauty shall linger, or a gnarled tree under which vermin shall gather. Saturday night is the cream of the week. The stamp affixed to our weekly deeds. A stepping-stone in the bed of the Great River. It is a round in the ladder leading to heaven or perdition. It is a tear which washes away the storms of the week, or burns its blistering way into the soul.

Let us rest to-night, weary toiler. Sit you down and be happy. Leave your head at your place of business, and bring your heart to the hearth and fender. Not your worldly heart, but the one yet fresh in memory. Sit by the fire, be it of coal or wood. What a battle life is! How few of us realize the warfare! We hardly know who our friends are. What a blessing that the grave has no eyes! How the hand of time closes its grasp to-night, bearing its wondrous gathering to God! What a medley to present to Him! Good acts and bad acts. Old age and childhood. Men, maids, and matrons—hopes, fears, promises kept and broken, hates, injuries, tears, sobs, sighs, smiles, rejoicings, pain, pleasure, sin, and goodness, all woven together like a tangled skein unravelled by a glance from that Wondrous Eye.

 * * * The hill is steep—its sides

are rough to the feet, and its tracks dangerous. Look back—down its slopes and juttings—over the memories of the past and into the vault of shadows wherein lie torn and bleeding the hopes which led you through the lanes of childhood into the broad road of life. Hope lives forever, but her children die one by one! Here and there they drop off as we toil upward to the great gate where stands a sentry of our own choosing.

  * * * Yet there is much to live for. Not for ourselves but for others. Humanity, in the integral, is but an infinitesimal sand, not worth living for. But we can live for others. Under a million roofs to-night, side by side sitting, are young hearts fitting out their frail barks for voyages on an ocean far more tempestuous than ever was the billowy waste grandly rolling its defiance between distant shores. Side by side to-night all over the land lovers sit, thankful that the labors of the week are ended, happy in turning and anticipating the apple the flavor of which is not yet fully known. Another downward turn to the light. Closer and yet closer the hearts as nearer come the chairs. The watch within us lays its seconds away—making up its bundle of shadows against another Saturday night.

 *   *   *   The sea of life is smoothed by love. Heart readings or attempts—lips meet—the summit is reached—the word is spoken—the apple is plucked, and life dates, not from birth, but from Saturday night.   *   *   *

 *   *   *   How fruits differ in flavor! Some are luscious to the taste. Some are dry, hard, tasteless, and unsatisfactory. Good to the eye, but a little indescribable something makes the beautiful apple but a cake of ashes. Life is an apple which is long growing but soon decays. Over the stepping-stones like this night, from the cradle so far on the road to the grave, we have carried our apple, waiting for a chance to eat it alone instead of dividing it with those who in turn would divide with us.

What is the influence that draws people into themselves and away from others? Whence comes the unseen hand that beckons hearts to wander off in the byways of solitude and live within little castles of their own building—cells of selfishness—instead of mixing with the crowd hurrying on, anxious to reach—*what?*

Why not look over the past, and guide better for the future from the resting-place given us by the clicking of the reel which marks His seconds —our weeks? There is so much done which ought not to have been done. So much left undone. Somehow the thread of life is wound up full of dirt and uneven places, no matter how straight and perfect we intend it to be. We reel it too fast. Down in the heart is a hidden power. Who of us all can solve the mystery? The heart is not a golden cloud, but a wide reach of prairie where grow some beautiful flowers—many delicate grasses—numerous gnarled shrubs fit only for ugly clubs, with here and there a fruit-bearing tree—a well from which others can drink—a bower where the weary can recline—a vine under which loved ones can sit—a lofty, firmly rooted oak, from whose branches climbers can see far out over the country—an occasional evergreen which will recall us to the minds of those who follow us from stone to stone on the way we all are wending.

* * * Let us pull up the shrubs which have no beauty — cultivate the flowers which breathe forth no fragrance, and plant the waste with vines—with trees which bear good fruit—with oaks rising high and strong, toying with the tempest and kissing the clouds rolling over them—with evergreens which shall mark our resting-place and cause others to say that we did not live in vain. Some of us can plant vines—some flowers—some tall trees—some of us the apple which shall be an apple of life—others the evergreen which shall keep the sun and storms from the marble visiting-card we invariably leave behind when going on the long journey. * * *

But to-night and to-morrow. Renew your love and energies against the trials of the unknown week. We would see all men happy. There are a million homes in the land where should be more happiness than there is, if men would but break away from the vice-like influences which surround them. Look back from to-night and then resolve for the future. Let the rich be more generous to the poor, and the poor be truer to themselves. There are too few homes—too many pictureless walls in the land. Rest to-night. Save the surplus earnings of the week, hard-palmed, honest laborer, whose earnest friend we are, no matter what tongue you speak, or from what country you came.

A thousand kind words might have been spoken, but were not. A thousand little luxuries might have been bought, but you would not thus use your earnings. Into the cesspool of revelry glides many a week of labor, leaving poverty, want, sickness, and unhappiness where should be love, plenty, and contentment. If for no one else, be a man for your own sake. Do right for the golden reward it always brings. Be a man. Stand and let the crowd rush on to the breakers which line the far shores of dissipation and careless expenditures. Begin the week with money in your pocket—happiness in your heart—the smiles of those around you—the good wishes of friends—the glorious renewal of faith in life which results from being a man. Then you will enjoy many others as you should and will this SATURDAY NIGHT.

CHAPTER XXXVII.

Happy New Year.

T is midnight! Like a strange dream, warped with troubles and woofed with blood, the year eighteen hundred and sixty-five has vanished over the brink of the GREAT PRECIPICE and around the corner—the bend in the stream of time—with merry bells we hear the coming of the Happy New Year. Still clinging to the bank while so many have gone by and down forever, waiting for the wave which shall unloose our hold, let us, in fancy, weave a mantle of silk from the dirty, blood-stained rags of

the past, thrown aside as the annual tyrant leaped into the pit of his own making, and let us also moss-plant the bank whereon we sit and wait for the leap to the echoless shore.

How like a strange dream! How the shadows of the past rise before us to warn or bless, as we who live traced our acts on the hard steel of memory's plate. Over the land there lies a mantle of snow, white as the forgiveness of GOD, as if lowered from the cerulean dome to teach man that most beautiful of all lessons. The snow covers the earth. The dark spots and ugly places are hidden beneath the Great Mantle, and the New Year comes to us, clad in the garment of peace once again.

HAPPY NEW YEAR! How unlike its predecessor, which has left on the heart so many and varied pictures of life, death, sorrow, and happiness! How many the changes one brief year has wrought! This is GOD's Saturday night—the closing of one of His weeks, with its millions of histories woven into a record for the future, from the gossamer of the present, as it floated by like meaningless froth on foaming billows.

One short year! It seems but like yesterday since we stood at the christening of the one now dead, and on its threshold laid our varied gifts—a bundle of plans, hopes, promises, and expectations for that future so many are ever dreading:

The lovers have forgotten the birthday of the year now dead, and the hopes they in love ushered in when the bells rang out the Happy New Year. The bashful boy—the wooing man, have stepped forth on the deck of the wondrous boat. The blushing girl, with implicit trust in plighted faith, careless of all save the love of her chosen one, has become a bride. Dark storms have howled down the aisles of her heart—happy indeed if her shelter proved true. There is a bravery in walking the plank—in leading a forlorn hope — in looking into the mouth of a cannon — but there is no braver act than for a trusting girl to cut loose from the hallowed port of parental protection and, relying on a simple "yes," launch her bark toward the shore of eternity in the search for that happiness every heart craves—so few discover.

The bride has in the year just dead become a widow, and with breaking heart gone into a grave deeper and darker than the one wherein rests her hopes. The groom has buried the one chosen from all of God's millions. The father has laid his darling boy beneath the sod—the mother has prayed God to spare, for ever so brief a time, the loved one who is not lost. The infant whose breath had hardly been given, marks an angelic chrysalis in the cold graveyard, while the pretty playthings of the child whose prattling and rompings gave joy to the household are sacredly put out of sight, in some secluded spot, to call forth floods of tears when none but grief and God are nigh.

Those who loved have been wronged—betrayed—forgotten vows have been kept or broken as destiny moved its wand. Homes have been made joyous and desolate during the reign of the monarch for whose death no one thinks to weep. Heart histories, to be read only in the land of the leal, have been written. We have locked many a secret in our hearts—or given them to the winds—men and women have been lost and saved—hearts have become cold, estranged and reckless, or made to know the power of love and kindness since last we wished those we met a HAPPY NEW YEAR.

There are pictures on memoric plates to-night each will do well to recall. Who of us have been true to our vows, our promises, our loves, our manhood, ourselves? God only knows. The beautiful picture we began to paint one year ago is marred by too many blots and punctures. There are too many stains on the mantle of life—too many links missing in our chain of good acts—too many weeds have grown up and gone to seed, in the plat we intended for flowers alone.

As GOD had wished us a Happy New Year and thrown His mantle over the earth, covering from sight the dark spots—the uneven places—the crooked sticks, sharp-cutting stones, and treacherous swamps, so let us who live throw the mantle of forgiveness over all men and stand erect before GOD and the world, thus proving our title to true manhood. Let us forgive those who have wronged us. It is not worth while for us to *hate* when so few years are given us.for *love*, before we enter upon the work of the future set apart for us. Let those who have wronged us be forgiven—let our loves and good intentions be strengthened, that our hearts may be lighter and the bank we sit on while waiting be beautified. Even brutes forgive and forget—surely man can do as much.

Not alone to the rich and prosperous—to those who wrap in furs to keep the cold out—in selfishness to keep the good in; who ride in luxurious coaches and display the labor of others in jewelry and fine apparel;—not alone to those who sip of costly wines—who rest on slumber-wooing couches—who sleep in embroidery — who revel in the delights wealth brings—who sit on well-rugged hearth by plated fenders, or feel the warm breath from glowing furnace—not alone to those who lack not for friends and enjoyment.

But to all. To the widow in her weeds—the orphan in rags—the child of poverty whose rest from toil never comes — to the noble-hearted watcher by the couch of suffering as well as to the sufferer wherever that sufferer may be—to the lonely of heart—the wrecked voyager on the terrible ocean of life—to the one who hungers for love—to the fallen and forsaken, the betrayed and wronged—the poor laborer whose hand is hard, but whose heart is true and warm—to those who sit by the home fire, be it ever so scant or humble—to honest-hearted laborers and those who mourn for loved ones lost in sickness or slain in battle—to those whose hearts are sad and whose joys are like dews of morning—to the poor and lonely who are always floating by upon the mystic river on whose bank we sit, do we wish from an earnest heart, a HAPPY NEW YEAR.

As the current rolls on may they land on green banks instead of broken points of rocks, to be cut and torn by the winds of adversity—amid fragrant groves beautified by the flowers of kind acts instead of a golgotha of sunken hopes—on islands ever green with love and affection—beneath spreading palms rather than on Arctic shores to shiver in the gales of adversity, borne on the wings of selfishness—with the living and loving rather than with those who are dead to that which makes life happy.

Soon will the brink be reached, the last look to the shore be given; and as those who watch the ripple turn away with a shudder to look again and find us gone forever, may the momentum given by a current strong and deep from good actions and noble impulses, carry us to the calm depth of an open sea, and not leave us impaled on the points and jutting rocks of disappointment, which, covered with victims, mark the dangerous shores which but line the current beyond safe for the true and the leal.

Look down the aisle. Throw open the blinds. Let the sunlight of true manhood in upon our hearts. Strive for the liberality which lifts man to a higher plane, and let us go forth battling with the army of cares with more of God and less of selfishness in our hearts.

Hold the dear ones and the loved ones closer to the heart—open the hand of charity and benevolence, and wipe out the dark spots of the past year with the good born from noble impulses of the new year, that it may indeed be a happy and a prosperous one.

CHAPTER XXXVIII.

Saturday Night.

ANOTHER week has been called in. Another seven-day net of providences has been reeled upon the invisible, and its wondrous haul of good deeds and bad pass in review before the Power of powers, the Great Father of all. A few more Saturday nights for us—perhaps no more for many who will read this article—it may be no more for the weary, hard, and tired brain but for which this little summing up would not be made.

It is good to rest, and we are glad to have one

night of the week for review. One night in which to look back at the hollowness of life— one little season in which we can look at the beautiful of it; for there is beauty in it, though the terrible to-morrow which promises more than it brings, sadly hides the perfection of days, life, and events.

Since last we sat by the desk to write thus outside of politics or business, there have been many changes. Many a heart has been widowed, and many a sad pillow in the final earthly home marks where sleep the missed ones. Do you know there is something very strange about this life and death ? We do not see why people so desire to live. From the cradle to the grave it is but toil, labor, sorrow, disappointment, and vexation. Were it not that we look for *to-morrow* to bring us happiness, or next week or next year to bring us comfort, there would be but dark clouds over all of us. The days, the years, are but the seconds and moments of GOD ! That

of time we prize so highly is of no moment to
Him, and yet how we hang on the great pendulum with its fifty-two figures thereon, each like this of which we write.

Death is not dreadful. It is but the sleeping here, to waken there? It is but sinking to rest in our office, when wearied with the labors of the day, and waking *at home*, where about us will stand in the sunshine of GOD's wondrous love the dear ones gone before to prepare the parlor of Eternity for your use and our resting, forever! And who would fear to thus sleep—to lay by the pen, to shove back from the desk and say " Good-by, wearying labors, we part forever"—to recline the head on back of cushioned chair, to smile as our eyes see the loved ones waiting, and to know that instead of walking we are wafted silently and on wings of love lest we waken before the glad surprise!

Working man and brother, we care not what your language, or how much you differ from us in opinion, to you we talk to-night. Opinions are but opinions. We may be wrong, you may be wrong—each of us may be wrong, for none but God is right. You have a right to your ideas—we have a right to ours, for they are all born of a higher power, to be operated on by acts, events, and arguments. But we would add to your happiness, here. Another will care for you in the Hereafter, as He will care for all of us. You teach us by your daily example many things. We see you nobly striving, and would help you if such thing can be.

We all seek happiness. Let us see how it can be had. You are tired. Then rest. Go home and be with those who are with you and of you. Throw your labor and dignity behind you. Open your heart. Talk of the beauties of the past you have seen, and congratulate yourselves that so much misery which has befallen others has escaped you. No matter how hard your lot, some one has a harder one. Think if there are not near you those you would on no account change places with.

If you love, love more. If you hate, hate less. Life is too short to spend in hating any one. Why war against a mortal who is going the same road with us? Why not expand the flower of life and happiness by learning to love, by teaching those who are near and dear the beautiful lesson? Your hands may be hard, but your hearts need not be. Your forms may be bent or ugly, but do you not know that the most beautiful flowers often grow in the most rugged, unsheltered places? The palace for care—the cottage for love. Not that there is no love in the mansion; but somehow if we are not very careful, business will crowd all there is of beauty out of the heart. This is why God has given Sabbaths and Saturday nights, that we may leave business in the office and have a heart-cleaning.

Forgive, as you would be forgiven. Love, as

you would be loved. Do as you would be done by. Suppose you were a weary prisoner at home, and think how welcome would be the coming of her you love, to be with you one night, if not each night, and go by the places of dissipation, of wickedness, where people would not so congregate if they did not *forget.* If you would have home happy, try to make it so. Light the lamp of life and keep it filled with the oil of love, care, affection, tenderness, and caresses, that it may not go to sleep in the dark when the work of life is ended. Children often fear to go to sleep in the dark, but there is another sleep, and a more terrible darkness! Only this, and nothing more!

Suppose we fall asleep in the office this Saturday night, and, neglecting to have trimmed our lamp, awaken to find but darkness and gloom, and uncertainty. We may find matches, but of what avail if there be no oil? We may *die* and live again, but if there be no lamps of love to lighten our future, better that we lived, even in sorrow.

Home can be happy if we make it so. Do not expect to cull all the flowers. Do not, simply to please yourself! We repeat—do not, simply to please yourself, for therein lies the shroud of happiness! Give, as is given. Keep back the bitter words. Others may be weary and bitter. Words unspoken are never remembered!

Go home to-night. If you would be happy, go home. If there is no happiness there take some, and kindle more. Save your earnings. Beautify your resting-places. Keep your heart warm and your brain steady. Save rather than waste, for the days go by faster than we dream, and want may overtake us, as it has others who lost the week in the great whirlpool of *Saturday night*.—" BRICK" POMEROY.

THE END.

NEW BOOKS
And New Editions Recently Published by
G. W. CARLETON & CO.,
NEW YORK.

GEORGE W. CARLETON.   HENRY S. ALLEN.

N.B.—THE PUBLISHERS, upon receipt of the price in advance, will send any of the following Books by mail, POSTAGE FREE, to any part of the United States. This convenient and very safe mode may be adopted when the neighboring Booksellers are not supplied with the desired work. State name and address in full.

Victor Hugo.

LES MISÉRABLES.—The celebrated novel. One large 8vo volume, paper covers, $2.00 ; . . . cloth bound, $2.50
LES MISÉRABLES.—In the Spanish language. Fine 8vo. edition, two vols., paper covers, $4.00 ; . . cloth bound, $5.00
JARGAL.—A new novel. Illustrated. . 12mo. cloth, $1.75
THE LIFE OF VICTOR HUGO.—By himself. . 8vo. cloth, $1.75

Miss Muloch.

JOHN HALIFAX.—A novel. With illustration. 12mo. cloth, $1.75
A LIFE FOR A LIFE.— . do. do. $1.75

Charlotte Bronte (Currer Bell).

JANE EYRE.—A novel. With illustration. 12mo. cloth, $1.75
THE PROFESSOR.— do. . do. . do. $1.75
SHIRLEY.— . do. . do. . do. $1.75
VILLETTE.— . do. . do. . do. $1.75

Hand-Books of Society.

THE HABITS OF GOOD SOCIETY; with thoughts, hints, and anecdotes, concerning nice points of taste, good manners, and the art of making oneself agreeable. The most entertaining work of the kind. . . . 12mo. cloth, $1.75
THE ART OF CONVERSATION.—With directions for self-culture. A sensible and instructive work, that ought to be in the hands of every one who wishes to be either an agreeable talker or listener. . . . 12mo. cloth, $1.50
THE ART OF AMUSING.—Graceful arts, games, tricks, and charades, intended to amuse everybody. With suggestions for private theatricals, tableaux, parlor and family amusements. Nearly 150 illustrative pictures. . 12mo. cloth, $2.00

Robinson Crusoe.

A handsome illustrated edition, complete. 12mo. cloth, $1.50

LIST OF BOOKS PUBLISHED

Mrs. Mary J. Holmes' Works.

'LENA RIVERS.—	A novel.	12mo. cloth,	$1.50
DARKNESS AND DAYLIGHT.—	do.	do.	$1.50
TEMPEST AND SUNSHINE.—	do.	do.	$1.50
MARIAN GREY.—	do.	do.	$1.50
MEADOW BROOK.—	do.	do.	$1.50
ENGLISH ORPHANS.—	do.	do.	$1.50
DORA DEANE.—	do.	do.	$1.50
COUSIN MAUDE.—	do.	do.	$1.50
HOMESTEAD ON THE HILLSIDE.—	do.	do.	$1.50
HUGH WORTHINGTON.—	do.	do.	$1.50
THE CAMERON PRIDE.—*Just Published.*		do.	$1.50

Artemus Ward.

HIS BOOK.—The first collection of humorous writings by A. Ward. Full of comic illustrations.   12mo. cloth, $1.50
HIS TRAVELS.—A comic volume of Indian and Mormon adventures. With laughable illustrations.   12mo. cloth, $1.50
IN LONDON.—A new book containing Ward's comic *Punch* letters, and other papers. Illustrated.   12mo. cloth, $1.50

Miss Augusta J. Evans.

BEULAH.—A novel of great power.			12mo. cloth,	$1.75
MACARIA.—	do.	do.	do.	$1.75
ST. ELMO.—	do.	do. *Just published.*	do.	$2.00

By the Author of "Rutledge."

RUTLEDGE.—A deeply interesting novel.		12mo. cloth,	$1.75
THE SUTHERLANDS.—	do.	do.	$1.75
FRANK WARRINGTON.—	do.	do.	$1.75
ST. PHILIP'S.—	do.	do.	$1.75
LOUIE'S LAST TERM AT ST. MARY'S.—		do.	$1.75
ROUNDHEARTS AND OTHER STORIES.—For children.		do.	$1.75
A ROSARY FOR LENT.—Devotional readings.		do.	$1.75

J. Cordy Jeaffreson.

A BOOK ABOUT LAWYERS.—Reprinted from the late English Edition. Intensely interesting.   12mo. cloth, $2.00

Allan Grant.

LOVE IN LETTERS.—A fascinating book of love-letters from celebrated and notorious persons.   12mo. cloth, $2.00

Algernon Charles Swinburne.

LAUS VENERIS—and other Poems and Ballads. 12mo. cloth, $1.75

Geo. W. Carleton.

OUR ARTIST IN CUBA.—A humorous volume of travel; with fifty comic illustrations by the author.   12mo. cloth, $1.50
OUR ARTIST IN PERU.—   do.   do. $1.50

www.ingramcontent.com/pod-product-compliance
Lightning Source LLC
Chambersburg PA
CBHW032105220426
43664CB00008B/1135